Chill Out and Cheer Up:
A Ten-Step Guide

Grace Grossmann

Yellow Scribe

Yellow Scribe Ltd.
London, UK

www.yellowscribe.co.uk

This paperback edition 2021

1

First published in Great Britain by
Yellow Scribe 2020

First published in Germany by
Yellow Scribe 2020

Copyright © Grace Grossmann 2021

Grace Grossmann asserts the moral right to be identified as the author of this work.

ISBN: 9798580957760

All rights reserved. No part of this publication may be reproduced, stored in a retrieval system, or transmitted in any form or by any means.

Contents

Contents	**3**
Introduction	**4**
Pressure	**11**
Positive Thinking	**47**
Doubt	**87**
Fear	**119**
Greed	**151**
Little Things	**187**
Nature	**227**
Connection	**261**
Solitude	**313**
Learn to love yourself	**356**
Acknowledgements	**409**

Introduction

Nowadays, we question what leading a happy life entails, how to *be satisfied*. We end up wasting our energy away, looking for happiness and not *living it the right way*. What even is the right way!? We follow the path that is supposedly set out to us by societal stresses and cunning commercials, steering us in the direction of Always. Wanting. More. When in your twenties, thirties, even sixties, we often question what's happening. Let's heal together.

We strive to be successful. We are compelled to work harder to earn more money and keep up with the standards of life set out in the Western world. We are forced to feel fulfilled by consuming, buying, investing, and all the while forget to invest time into ourselves.

We are fed false beliefs about the way we should look, led on not to feel comfortable in our own skin. It's a constant catch 22 effect.

We are misinformed by the media to believe every word they say, consistently washing our screens with negative news and reasons to fix our insecurities and live our dream. We are tormented by social media platforms to seek out short-term gratification and propelled to "live our best life".

We are reliant on drug doses instead of natural highs. We are addicted to technology, TV and anything that temporarily numbs our mind. We choose to aimlessly scroll through our news feed rather than interact with one another.

We are living in the future, regretting the past when all we have is now. We are allowing the past to build our identity, instead of permitting ourselves to let go of who we were and be who we are in this moment. We are forced to not feel by the world we created and its magnitude of sin that surrounds us. We are shattered because society stuffs itself with every last piece of our hope.

Every minute we turn to feel judged, watched and criticised, countless times questioning who to trust. We must take a step back from the world and realise our potential, to enable love, joy and peace to seep through the cracks that we tape up with a false smile. Where is the love, joy and peace that is deeply stored within each and every one of us?

You are here for a reason, and you are important. So let's start with you.

Here's a bit about me:

I'm happy-go-lucky - and when I wrote this, I was living in Spain spending my time on cloud nine (if there was a cloud in sight there!).

Now editing the book, I'm in a **tricky** place. Although a yoga teacher and coach, I too can experience the dark.

I've been diagnosed with onset schizophrenia and depression so I can relate and you are not alone. Reality check: A really bad mental health phase can happen to anyone, even a person like me who wrote an entire book about cheering up.

If you're going through a bad time, don't hesitate to tell friends and family and seek professional help! We must work together to get better. I know I can't help everyone, but I can help someone and that is all that matters. You opening up is going to make your circle of care know that there is more than we think in the air.

We are all suffering one way or another. So if I can speak up, you can too. Together, let's remove the negative stigma around mental health, especially the stigma around clinic stays and medication, and seeking support (something I struggled with recently!

That concerned myself overcoming my own internalized stigma and then staying in a clinic for a few weeks.)

So mental health is more than positive toxicity, it's like a tree. As any tree, there are many branches that have different functionalities for the tree. Currently, I'm experiencing a part of the mental health tree to an extent I never envisioned. I'm in a deep depression and the onset of schizophrenia wherein I've lost control of my self-care, I truly am not *fully* there.

The way I'm getting out of it: *opening up to family and friends who have all showered me with an overwhelming amount of love and care.*

The way I'm getting out of it: *reminding myself that one step at a time counts.*

How I'm doing it: *forgiving myself daily and trying again, no matter how hard it gets (and trust me, I've laid in bed all day everyday for a while before I admitted something was wrong with me).*

So if you're reading this and suffering, don't suffer alone, because the people who care will be there. But for now, no pressure. Read this and release your dismissal.

Now then:

This is a book to guide you into becoming more aware and accepting of who you are and how you feel. It's a book for mental hygiene. **I'm Grace and I am here to inject your life with hope again, because life is worth living with a smile.**

Throughout this book, writing a list will be prompted whether thoughts flood in or not, so give yourself the time to take notes and take heed on what you are reading, for you to fully engage with this book.

Writing is a wonderful way to acknowledge how you are feeling and what you wish to work on within. To create self-love is the reason I wrote this book, so use these lists to *lighten up your life!*

Pressure

What is pressure?

The pressure is everywhere,
Like a thief in the night sparking fright, it takes away every last slice of delight.
The pressure pushes us to perceive ourselves as failures before even trying;
tells us to question if we are doing what everybody "expects" us to do,
social norms knock at our needs and tell us we must stick to the societal layout of life, or we end up on the streets.

Pressured through a plethora of precarious platforms, pushy people surrounding us every damn day.

The pressure is hard to escape,
It can push and pull us into shape,
Let's let it show us the light and love instead of going with the push and shove.

Pressure comes in many shapes and sizes, permitting it to fracture us in ways that we assume are out of our control when submitting to its strength.

The power of pressure affects our emotions, no matter how it takes hold of us.

Oh, pressure, how you influence our decisions, perplex prospects and distort or drive our dreams. Dear pressure, please become a friend, not a foe and let me seek out all I know.

Pressure affects us all. I feel it. Due to our wired world these days, the pressure is a part of daily life. We are taught to live with pressure from an early age, yet not to deal with it very well. Society thrives off pressuring people to consume, corrupting our judgment on what it is and how to overcome it, rather than succumb to it. Societal pressures convince us that following trends and embracing our ego is fine, when it does not serve our purpose to flourish and blossom at our progress, following our rhythm.

We are persuaded through pressure to stick to specific criteria laid out for us from our youth, all to feel fulfilled, settled and 'worthy'. Pressure ropes us in to be part of a rat race, making life into a competition. Pressure initiated by friends fantasies on the motive of fitting in, otherwise known as peer pressure. Strangers signal pressure, asserting us to feel the need to prove ourselves as an object rather than an entity. Loved ones pressure us to lead a life that should serve us to the best of our ability and beyond, interrogating our capability to continue.

At other times, our nearest and dearest pressure us to pursue a path that is predominantly attached to ambitions unaccomplished by themselves. Pressure in any size or shape is there; profound and can be found in every corner, either love or hate being the catalyst, causing confusion or motivation to take over. How many times have I said pressure now?

Ha. Ok, let's see how we can stop it getting to us.

Don't let the pressure get to you

Every branch of pressure is a battle to stay in control. Each pressure presents itself as a series of torn-up emotions, trying to torment with your balance in life. Pressure causes imbalance. However, there is always a wish to resist being pressured into new decisions, be it big or small… it is deep inside us all. I try to reach in for it when the pressure gets too much to deal with.

It is your intuition or your gut feeling; however you want to identify it. Listen to it. Find it and feel it. Eventually, if you surrender to the world's pressures, it will hoax your harmony into acting on whims with the outer world in mind, disregarding your inner world. As soon as the force takes hold of you, it automatically leads to distress and distorts every hint of happiness through self-doubt.

A heavy load of pressure is utterly hard to be relieved of if we allow ourselves to be consumed by all the feelings attached to it. Misidentify yourself with the forces (may the force not be with you haha), and you might just lose yourself. Nobody knows what's best for you other than yourself. Yet this is what we stumble upon. The struggle is real.

SO here's your first reminder:

It is OK. It is OK to feel like you are unsure of where you are going. It is OK not to know what you are doing. It is OK to feel the force of pressure placed on your shoulders, weighing you down, where outside resources seem the only feasible way out of the infinite insecurities of life. It is OK to not be OK.

Nobody is capable of being OK all the time, fluttering their wings like a fairy. We have all been there, it is only human to not feel OK. What is not OK, is to give in to the pressure and identify with its cunning ability to fade your true essence out. It is not OK to compromise and lose control of your life due to all the pressures that push you further away from what you believe in or aim to achieve.

It is not OK to let stress take you away from the bigger picture and focus on its confinement of suffocating feelings that compel unworthiness to linger and live within. It is not OK to let the pressure be a big part of your life, losing control of your own life all the while. Life is not given to us with a distinct destination, instead a path to find your route.

So, next time pressure pokes at your delicate state of confusion, cure the menace with optimism and openness to the unknown because that is the beautiful thing about life.

OK, so, the pressure is planted in our biological clock, meaning we must complete our aspirations and passions, within a certain amount of time because our days are numbered. (I don't mean to scare you!) Life is limited. Time is of the essence.

However, nobody knows what tomorrow will bring, so sometimes planning with pressure in mind can take you away from the now and fling you into the realms of the impending.

You never know, but pressure can urge us to be in control. Sorry to say, but you are not in control. Nobody is. As much as we would like to control specific outcomes or prospects, control cannot be guaranteed in life. That is a given.

There is a point in your life after giving in to society's demands and people's pressures, where you may doubt your decisions and question what you have genuinely done for your pleasure. We must realise joy prompts us to advance in a more fulfilling life because it involves simply sticking to what you want to do.

Pleasure *signifies* serving yourself and being the best you, delight in this context is following your heart.

Remove pressure to prosper in finding out what makes you tick, and tackle life at your best capacity, full of courage and charisma. Pleasure is exclusive, in the way each person experiences it in their own peculiar and precious ways. I am talking about organic happiness, not based upon any conditions promised to meet all your needs, yet pleasure that comes naturally, untouched by superficial boundaries based on false promises.

Unfortunately, it is not as easy as A, B, C because society has had a 1, 2, and 3 all over our freedom of choice. (You got it? Good!) Weirdly enough, we are made to feel worthless when we don't go with the flow that is outlined for us, where landing a career or becoming an influencer seems to have slithered its way through to be one of the immense pressures yet. Right now, we are suffering from the stress of power.

The power is currently driven in a marketing manic world, haunting us in our homes; a place where we should feel at ease, and sneaking up on us on the street; a place where we should feel safe, or at least expect to. Marketing makes us feel like shit; there is no doubt about it. The marketing hype of advertisements has always been out there to bring us down, so we become dependent on consumerist resources to feel complete.

Advertising sells us an illusion, so that we see things like a gate to happiness, hoping we have a chance of opening it up and entering into this man-made madness; an answer to all our prayers. It compels us to cling on to things that are fake and only brings short-term fulfilment. This power is surging across our webpages, television screens, bus stops.

It has taken over like a tsunami and won't leave us alone. Everywhere we go, the pressure is following us in the form of marketing. It is an absolute materialistic driven demeanour, determined to deliver us into a reliance on the outer world for happiness.

We are now bringing children into a world that will make them feel bad for going outside the social norm, wanting more than ever before. Take a minute to realise when looking at these ads and fads; you are worth much more than they are. You are worthy. Try not to obey or be dismayed by what the capitalist society is pushing you towards – a pressure involving money and more money, in a relentless rally of destroying the world simultaneously. Think about it before you buy it. Look at it properly before you click and purchase.

Take time to know what you want before you comply with consuming and tune in to your power that does not include a shower of signals for you to devour in disengagement. Eventually, marketing will destroy you, and you will become blind to what matters. You matter, we all matter, so we must steer away from the pressure to latch on to products and become aware that we need to be responsible for our actions.

The pressure got to me, as it does with everyone at some point.

As a young person after graduating University, I felt the effect of pressure pile itself on me like a load of washing thrown to the corner of your room for weeks. The smell turns into a stench. A stench of stress induced by endless questions and concerns that cause you to feel bewildered and baffled by life.

We go through the whole hoax of the education system with a predetermined promise of a brighter future, when at the end, you are left in the dark questioning "now what?"... well, at least I did. Then we question why there is a peak in so many young people suffering from mental health issues. Wake up and smell the coffee. The coffee that is given to us to always be on the ball and battle for the best opportunities on the ladder to success, but where can this ladder lead to and does the top even exist? No.

We strive to succeed because failure is forbidden and frowned upon, especially if you do not have a profession or passion in mind. We get lost in the puzzling path of further education because the system says if we are well educated, then we will prosper in life. In reality, we are left with a loan that will probably never be paid off and a state of stress that will probably send us to a therapist.

OK, so education is wonderful. We should never dismiss it or take it for granted; however, how we may depend upon it for fulfilment is far from reality. We are all told what to learn, what is essential to know what we should know etc. for us to distinguish our choice of profession. What about classes about taxes and real things in the real world we need to know?! Time changes, and so do perspectives. Time changes and so do our priorities as a human race when it comes to worldly matters.

We are currently suffering some of the greatest threats on Earth – climate change and Covid. If you choose to believe it or not, either way, our world is going kaput. Hurricanes, floods, plastic pollution, the lot is a heavy burden to us all. However, some people are still prioritising other shitty pressures. Through time and experience, our thoughts and passions permanently are a product of love, loss and living. At the end of it, we have no clue what we want to do.

We are therefore made to feel like a failure before we have even done anything except being part of the education system. Such societal influenced pressures participate in the making of mental health issues because we are pushing aside our health, well-being and dreams. There is an excellent effort in removing mental health as a stigma in society, and rightly so, but sometimes feeling alone is spurred on by society's pressure that pushes our emotions aside, treating us like robots trapped in a system that decides for us to follow the masses.

It does not engage with our inner light, yet rather dismisses our right of speech and deters us from what is real. It engages with our egoism and relies on our hope to put a mortgage down. *This kind of pressure prolongs distorted emotions and casts aside our courage that should be about discovering who we are and how we can cope, rather than how to carry on regardless of how we ultimately feel*. As suicidal rates continue to rise significantly, we should be concentrating on society's powerful force and how to deal with these mixed up emotions that are causing grief by putting us on guard.

Whilst people are being buried under pressure, bizarrely, the public doesn't realise the missing piece. The missing part of the puzzle starts with you and ends with you. We should wake up and rise above the conditions that society has set out for us, supporting each other in removing them and participating in kindness. It is time to make a change. Try things out and be thankful for every experience, opportunity and moment. Even if you aren't where you want to be, there is nowhere you should be.

Every little thing lets you grow in one way or another, it is up to you to honour yourself and not allow others to determine your destiny for you. Remind yourself this when pressure pounds on your present moment. Everything takes time, so stop being so hard on yourself. Grow where you've got to grow, go when you gotta go. Self-acceptance is a process. A process is prioritising change, allowing growth and surrendering yourself to go slow. Permit yourself to ponder on what you prioritise. Give yourself permission to let go of the pressures battering you left, right and centre. Use the lesson of pressure to effectively push you in the right direction of seeking out self-love and self-acceptance, rather than pulling you in to feel feeble and frightened about your own choices in life.

What are you going to do now? Where are you going? Just two of the incessant questions that stay by your side, like a young child asking their parent for that toy ever since seeing the advert for it. So, what did I do? I escaped to Spain. It seemed the perfect option for me, back to a chilled life in Seville, but I still felt pressure from all my friend's different decisions detaining my delights in life to go with the flow. It was OK because it made me realise how we all had contrasting career goals, instead, I allowed it to show me that I am where I want to be.

There is nowhere you shouldn't be (remember that!)

Going through University never jerked me to think realistically of where I want to be in 5 years, I mean who knows? It hit me all of a sudden. This whole five year plan is always pushed upon us and it may be good for some, not for others. Don't make yourself feel bad for not having one. The waves of adulthood, like real-life tax, rent, adult strains came crashing down on me. Shit, I didn't want to grow up! All along, we want to be an adult and can't wait to get that job and be fully independent, but it isn't what it's hyped up to be at the beginning.

Nobody helps you unless you are fortunate to be blessed with beautiful parents like I am, but still, you are left in the lurch on how to pay taxes and important stuff like that. So taking myself out of the pressure ridden world in the UK and running to Spain at least showed me I want to do what is right for me and go with my heart and not what society shoves me to think is right for me.

From a young age, we are expected to know what "position" we want to be within society. Do we ever know? Erm no!! We are all just trying to be something instead of nothing. We are taught to have an idea about what we want to do from our early years, prodded at constantly to be positioned as a person in society. "What do you want to be when you grow up?", one of the most common questions if not the most commonly asked as a child.

Well, guess what? The answer is ever-changing, unpredictable, shifting as one grows up and gets to know themselves better. Don't attach yourself to labelling yourself. It may be uncertain and fluctuating until your senior days because we are learning more and more about ourselves daily, if open and ready to develop with one's desires and divinity.

For example, I had no idea I wanted to write this book until my best friend suddenly passed away 3 years ago and I thought:

I need to write a book primarily aimed at the quarter-life crew, so they know they are not alone through and through.

Ever since, I can't stop writing and would love to keep going. Back to the point: we are all suffering in some way or other from worldly pressures. It's OK, accept and move on, don't hold on and be in agony.

One of the first questions, if not the first, is "what do you do?" when meeting someone. "What do you do for a living?" may be a better phrase because I honestly came to detest being asked this question, as if your whole characterisation depends on it. Who cares if you're a teacher, you're a lawyer or a cleaner, what matters the most is you, as you are. No conditioning, just you. Your passion, your smile, your laughter, your look.

You may be thinking, well some people are blessed to be working their passion and there are only a handful of humans who are lucky to do so. That is not the case.

Now more than ever, we have opened ourselves up to a nomadic style of life through the means of the internet – use it to grasp your potential and gain essential insight into your likes and dislikes. The positions are infinite on the internet, and new job positions are being created every day! Not to say you have to follow your passion for a living, but give something a go. See, there is a positive in the world wide web, you just have to find it. Google it ;)

The expectancy embedded within this question of "what do you do?" causes us to feel frail and crack at the pressure because society has shoved us into a queue of confusion. Don't let it stress you; let it light your spirit. See how you answer, listen to what you say, and be truthful with yourself. It is no mystery that you cannot see with no tint a lot of the time. We are in a time of labelling.

Label this, tag that. Who cares? Do not limit yourself to your job title, instead be open to the process of pursuing your passion. Everything takes time. We are all put into a system where our passionateness modifies with time, travelling, teaching. Why should we be in desperate haste to succeed straight away?

If you don't "keep up" with companions or colleagues, that is only because you are comparing yourself. Let them go with their rhythm of music and manage your mix in an open and honourable style. Respect your timing and allow yourself time to grow, bloom and flourish along the way. Take precautions, take care of your thoughts, consider yourself! Take chances. Endeavour in what you want because it does not mean a thing if you are not progressing at the rate of your pals or people of your age; everyone is different. Personal progress is something sometimes not seen by others, it is individualised.

Dedicate time and effort to what makes you thrive and feel alive, rather than what others fool you into feeling momentarily doped upon. Focus your will on what is within and you will shine from without. Your purpose will elevate you to achieve what you have set out in your mind to reach. Write it down. Consider time to be on your side, use it mindfully. Let time stimulate you by what you aim to achieve.

Pressure can be good!

Pressure can be off-putting, but sometimes it can also be considered as a positive. Like everything in life, it's good to maintain balance. With the bad, also comes good.

A spoonful of pressure may provide us with determination and drive at times. Pressure can be a condition that urges us to become more present in our process of work and life.

For example, pressure can make people work well under a time limit. At University, I felt like the closer the deadline, the better I'd work because I thought the force compelling me to complete the task at hand. However, the load would take its toll, and stress would seep its way through the burden that brought self-doubt rise to the top.

The realisation of having to complete tasks under a limited time frame may not be the most effective way for some people, as the tension mounts up and makes you feel worn out, for others, it might have a powerful effect on concentration. Either way, pressure can be critical in the equation of motivation now and then. It can be portrayed as a perk in progress.

We will always feel life pressures, but they can be utilised in a way to assert yourself better. The pressure is an incentive to prove yourself. The pressure pushes us to make moves and pursue plans. It is a healthy gratuity when wanting to prove yourself, but it can become dangerous if served as a reason to prove yourself "worthy" to others.

Employing pressure to disrupt balance and focus on someone else's priorities, means you will never be able to win the battle against pressure. For example, suppose pressure lets you lean on another person's precedence. What you find important in life will become obscured, letting the load mislead your direction, ultimately making them the priority and not you. It's great to have people to look up to, follow in their footsteps, but make your mark.

If you are easily misguided when making decisions based on others provoking you, then notice that it is not for your will, but theirs. Say no. We don't say it enough and are always inclined to serve others, but what about serving yourself? Aim to say no more often. Some people might want what is best for you, but personal pressures can only guide you if harmony is in mind. We must treat pressure with priority when it concerns defining what is important to us and what pressures can assist you in life. Thus, allow pressure to guide you, in place of guilt-tripping you into a life that does not follow your heart.

So it can be seen that pressure presents itself to you to carry on and complete stages in life, that otherwise might not be reached if pressure didn't push you forward. There is, however, a risk that it can bring you back because stress can be hard to cope with. Procrastinating can seem so much easier to do, especially when you don't know what to do. Escaping from pressure involves hiding away from reality, as the physical force can weigh you down into deep darkness of desperation and depression. Giving in to pressure like this, will take control of your life so that it does not seem worth living for any more.

In this case, we put pressure at the back of our mind to escape it. At times uninvited, the force will find its way and burst out unexpectedly, leaving us loaded with a miserable concoction of feelings congesting our clear view to move on. It may make us feel lost and incomplete, due to its ability to wrap itself around us and control the tide of emotions washing you with stress and anxiety.

This is where we must identify the root of the pressure and what exactly is supporting it to stay as a substance in life.

1. **WHAT** is sustaining your pressure?
2. **WHO** is spurring it on?
3. **WHY** is it noticeable?
4. **WHERE** did the pressure come from?
5. **WHEN** did it make me feel like this?

Ask yourself the five W's! Notice the problem it is causing, so that the root may be removed before it becomes harder to extract and intertwine with the roots of your regrets. Like any other problem in life, once you are aware of it, you have the responsibility to remove it. You have a choice to be who you want to be, therefore you have a choice to acknowledge pressure and get rid. As every other sensibility, we are gifted to glance at it and let go.

As long as we are aware of where it originated, then can we participate in defeating it to feel free. If we combat the pressures of the world by accepting that we can't escape them, then the pressure will not take centre stage in your life any longer.

Instead, your vitality and well-being will be at the forefront with the prime focus set on your own needs. Subsequently, pressures will be seen as a mere product of our society, irrelevant for you to take seriously.

Cure pressure...

Cure pressure for patience. At the minute, pressure predominantly arises through social media. Platforms pull us in, and some sort of pressure is guaranteed every time we check our feed, evoking emotions that eat us up.

Social media forces us to feel like we need to live up to some sort of standard and expectation, mostly set by the people who are in the limelight with lots of followers. However, these emotions evoke a need to live up to an imaginary regulation, solely initiated by our messed up mindset conceived from the forces. Don't let yourself be taken down by the pressure, pulling you at every string of self-love; we should grasp on to them to gain clarity. Don't let your mind drift with the unforeseen and be taken away by daydreams instigated by Instagram photos portraying scenes that are purposefully posted to make you feel down, compare yourself, torment your decisions. Don't let it. Take hold of it.

For example, every time you enter the bubble of Instagram and some people's photos compel you to compare and despair, so you sit there yearning for a holiday, I mean how else are you supposed to feel other than envy?

This pressure preoccupies your mind, making you feel like you should go away and escape everything, questioning 'why is this my life and not what is sprayed all over social media?'

How do you know that person is pleased?

    A picture says a lot, but it also says nothing. It could all be lies, and the person behind the screen is seeking out acceptance through likes and comments. This pressure proclaims discomfort and rage, from the fact that you are not living the lavish life you deserve. **FOMO sets in motion**. It's simply not fair. The spiral of sad emotions starts to stir throughout your mind and body, causing stress and sadness, lowering self-esteem and grating at your confidence.

    Combat this feeling and cut down the time you spend on social media, cut out the people you follow that don't make you feel good and start following others that inspire ambition and show you motivation. Consider yourself and your life, remembering everything takes time. Inhale and exhale. Be patient with yourself and do things that will bring you back to real-time and the real you.

Take a bath. Take a walk. Take a break from all the bullshit we are constantly bombarded with; nobody is perfect.

Cure pressure with acceptance.

The pressure is like a battle, only conquered when you learn to accept defeat or victory. Stop and stay still, recognise that everything is OK. I learnt to cure my post-uni pressure by getting where I am at. Once I realised that everyone does their own thing and I am doing mine, I started to change my mindset and learn from where I was at in the present moment, with whom I was getting to know, learning from them and learning from every day by taking one step at a time. At the time, I was teaching English, knowing that it wasn't what I wanted to pursue long-term, so I questioned myself, pressured myself, to start and make the best out of it.

Not to mention, I couldn't help compare myself to all my other friends that were thriving in their way. Coming to terms with the fact that I can make the best out of what I have got makes me more driven to excel in this opportunity and I made it an experience I learnt from in more ways than one. Learning to use pressure to prosper brings true potential into focus. There is always a possibility to switch your mindset and make the most of every situation you find yourself in.

Anyone can do it – if I did, so can you. Sometimes it seems people don't have to try so much because the best job has been given to them, a great spouse has been found for them, a great life has been handed to them on a plate... it is not the case.

Yet, we are easily marvelled by others and want what they have. Stop. Accept. Appreciate. Don't let other people's lives pressure you into a pit of self-pity, try to be happy for them and accept to learn from the life that you have been blessed with, instead of squandering over the life that is not yours.

Feeling worse about other people's lives is not worth your time nor breath. A lot of people participate in this act, and it baffles me, mainly because most of the time, the dream life displayed on Instagram is absolute bullshit! I find it all fake. This sort of pressure is misinterpreted in mind, so it feels like envy, jealousy etc., and it is a dangerous path of force to not be followed or supposed for lengthy times. Consider yourself and your life. Find things to feel grateful for, not involving money or madness; such sins will make us feel bad for being alive and challenge our right to be worthy in the world. You are worthy.

When you are aware of this, be happy for others lives and let it be. Acceptance is key. Patience is free. When pressure creeps up and makes you feel a hint of such cynical feelings, fight it off with confidence, charisma, and care. Care for who you want to be and don't care about who others want you to be. If you fall into this trap, you will never feel good enough.

Good enough does not exist, remember! The pressure is like a thief in the night- you cannot expect it, but you can beat it. Beat it up (let's not get violent, but you get the hint). It comes in disguise, uttered in ways we cannot predict or foresee.

Occasionally, it appears through people we think the world of, so we must be wary and watch our ways and days. Pressure comes in many shapes and sizes; it never ceases to leave us alone, unless we own our throne. Win pressure over and OWN IT.

Pressure takes on many forms

Pressure from the outer world will eat you up and spit you out. Peer pressure will provoke your dark side to dismiss your purpose and make you question why, doubting choices as well as your position in life. Pressure from strangers will disregard your destiny and lead you astray to disengage you from your interests. Pressure from loved ones lets us believe that we must be doing the right thing, although sometimes it is driven by the hope to succeed in their eyes. In general, the pressure that we feel in any shape or form lingers and does not leave unless we treat it with a concoction of care: a serving of self-love, sprinkle of courage and handful of optimism. We all face a myriad of life pressures, and it is possible to deal with them in a way to feel okay.

Learn to live with a humble heart; be grateful for what you have got so that pressure cannot corrupt your positive perspective. A hint of pessimism will only let the pressure progress and prolong the incompetent feeling to find a home in your heart.

Healthy pressure from yourself, however, may help you to succeed, if harnessed delicately. Feeling the crunch can provoke you to practice self-development and self-acceptance because you are becoming aware that pressure can compel you to press forward. I mean, it is impossible to go back to the past, so always remember it is onwards and upwards from here. *Play Moving on Up here!* Unhealthy pressure causes you to condone your true self by always focusing on the future, forgetting about now.

Stress can trigger pessimism in your character and flow of life. As long as you are aware of what type of pressure is being planted within you or thrown at you, then you can use it to your own accord and find ways in which you can deal with it, overcome it. The pressure is omnipresent and forever existent, meaning we can't escape it, but we can embrace it in a way that will spur us on to be the person we want to be. Let it leave and let yourself, love. Exchange pressure for pleasure.

Trade pressure for patience. Practice patience, so the pressure will shatter into shards of success and stability. Allow yourself time to deal with the pressures and be patient with yourself. Accept where you are at and stop comparing. Swap society's pressures for individual needs that will enhance your life in ways that will serve you and not sink you into a pit of penitence.

One thing we must remember is: **it is OK to feel pressured.**

Don't panic from pressure; **embrace it with acceptance.**

Don't panic from pressure; **take it as a lesson in self-development.**

Don't panic from pressure; **see it as a start to setting goals and getting on with life.**

Don't panic from pressure; **catch it before it latches on to you with unbearable feelings.**

Don't panic from pressure; **use it as a force for imagination.**

Push pressure away, don't let it be in the way.

Practice patience, practice love. Let go, look forward.

Positive Thinking

What is positive thinking?

"The happiness of your life depends upon the quality of your thoughts." - Marcus Aurelius.

Nowadays, our minds struggle to naturally think positively due to the daily stresses of life. Moreover, our brains are wired to be more negative than positive because of survival mode. Distractions. Options. Diversions.

Many mental blockages contribute to the misfortune that our minds cannot mould a healthy and optimistic logic. It is a battle for our brains to stay positive. Our natural negativity is stirred up through survival mode that constructs a way of thinking around feeling threatened.

It is only capable to access positivity through the navigation of stressful times, where our brains solely spurt out beams of brightness to keep us going. We are stronger than we think and our minds are on our side to keep the peace. Our brains are structured to see the world through a gloomy lens because of society's standards. However, our brain can change: it is up to us whether we choose to revel in positivity or stew in negativity.

Positive thinking is about will power. It entails caring for your thoughts by manifesting in an abundance of optimistic led deliberations, to uplift and make life flow like the way it should. In fact, (in case your hint of doubt just hit!) it is possible to "rewire" your brain to be happy by recalling three things you are grateful for every day, for a matter of 21 days.

Why 21 days, I hear you ask? Research shows that it is the amount of time required to "make a habit". In other words, it takes us three weeks to engage in a practice that will sooner rather than later, not be difficult to follow through with, because we become adjusted to it. It becomes our second nature.

When we partake in positive thinking, we see things in a different light, empowering us with an energy that enables us to take on life with a clear conscience. Gratitude. Honour. Splendour. Positive thinking involves seeing the positive over the negative. Positive thinking is understanding that tomorrow is a new day, yesterday is already behind you and today is the day your life begins.

Positive thinking is seeing the clouds and reckoning they will clear for the sun to shine through, rather than sanctioning rain to dampen down your day. It makes you smile. It shows you how to be grateful for little things. It prescribes you with a natural high. It puts a bounce in your stride. It favours an "at least" approach to situations, professing that things could be worse off. It is about counting your blessings.

Positive thinking is about taking on life with all its battles and bombshells, then turning it into balance and bliss. Positive thinking makes you deal with disappointment and heal with happiness. Positive thinking authorises you to see the good in people, with a hope to change the world by restoring faith in each other's ability and progress towards a better place we are proud to call home.

Positive thinking pushes our mental state forward to develop rather than decay. Positive thinking replenishes negative connotations with good intentions. Positive thinking takes you on a daily adventure of seeking long-term sustainable change through serendipitous schemes of self-care. Positive thinking lets go of the useless negative thoughts; mostly lies fed to us from a capitalist society driven to feed off of our imperfections, rather than triumph over our unique personalities.

Capitalism does not allow for individuality to thrive, but permits for egoistic vices to be alive. Positive thinking can be achieved by anyone and is accessible to those ready for a life to be fulfilled with happiness, prosperity, and gratitude. Positive thinking is a choice, so let us choose this route and remember nobody can be positive all the time!

Negative thinking is normal, not weird.

It is easy to fall into the trap of negative thoughts. It can snatch you out of seeing things for what they are, tainting them with pessimistic perceptions.

Negative thinking does not like glad tidings nor drifting with the daily pleasures of life. The thoughts prefer to grab you and take you under, drowning you with a haunting hangover ridden with anxiety (hangxiety). It rivals against any hint of optimism, with a fierce determination to bring you down by tormenting your mind with terrible chatter. This is known as self-talk, also acknowledged as the ceaseless stream of corrupt contemplations, otherwise known as thoughts racing through the mind. We have **6000** thoughts a day - what are you going to choose to think?

We are all troubled by pessimistic probing knots of nasty and gloomy views, up to the point of practically being taken over by them. We let them control us and that is where we go wrong. I've gone wrong many times with overthinking and allowing one thought to cloud my way all day. It's easily done - don't beat yourself up.

Yet discouraging self-talk can be halted, so that we can heal our stream of consciousness with an eagerness to promote well-being and protect our mental health, all through practice. When you practice something, it becomes a habit after some time, so practically speaking, nurturing your thoughts can become a ritual that may be applied at any point. What do they say? Practice makes perfect. If you can tackle the negative thoughts by not attaching yourself to them, then you can overcome the hardship of fooling your mind with negative thinking.

Don't worry – it is human nature for us to think negatively rather than positively. Our thoughts are enhanced by what and who we surround ourselves with, because in effect, they become a part of us. Human nature urges us to always think of the worst-case scenarios, so that we have a chance in finding safety and security through money-driven delusions, not getting to the root of the mind.

When I stopped being a student, I was suddenly an adult, who couldn't rely on student discount or crazy nights out where I could skip lectures (and life!). I couldn't just lie in bed because I was hungover and watch Netflix for the rest of my life (although I am sure everyone does this from time to time).

I was an adult, of whom had responsibilities and priorities to distinguish and manage.

This puzzle of perplexing emotions pushed me further away from positive thinking and caused me to stress. I found peace in practising yoga as a way to yield my energy and not be taken away by the world's pressures. Finding space and time is essential to heighten happy thoughts. Bake or cook. Read or write. Walk or run. Play football or tennis. Find what makes you feel good.

You-time will boost and encourage you to carry on – furthering the field of positive vibrations to manifest in being asserted, open, free from restraint. If obstacles obstruct the way, we trip up. It's OK.

Nobody can "ace" positive thinking, it is a personal thing. This is a part of prompting the present moment to preoccupy you, by maintaining the frame of mind that negative events are temporary and can be dealt with, therefore can be seen through until the light at the end of the tunnel. If this point is not contemplated, especially when confronted with a crisis, we are prodded and poked at with pessimism, scepticism, making it harder to resolve the situation.

We practice doubting ourselves and our worth, as well as others. We are embedded and entangled into negative thinking because simply put, our western world wants us to. We are expected to think of the worst when everything is going tits up (AKA bad!), so that we have a chance at feeling safe.

We prioritise perspectives that penalise our happiness over embracing a positive attitude, when in fact the act of complaining can torture our health and those around us. We complain because at that moment it feels good to release such sinister remarks; in the long run it rewires our brain for future complaining to become a regular occurrence.

We act out in malicious ways on some days when things aren't going your way because we are suffering and want everyone else to suffer with us. Nagging is draining, whereas admiring is inspiriting. Negative thinking concerns itself with a myriad of mentalities that mould us into harbouring poisonous personalities and ultimately making us a sour person.

Positive talk is harder to grasp when a negative perspective is covering the inner light up.

Heal with optimism

We must **treat** pessimism with **optimism**; for some might not be as easy to employ as others. It is, however, achievable for all. It is up to you to seek out positive self-talk because it is controlled by you. When put into practice, your emotions will prosper in positivity- always seeing the good in the bad. It is not about ignoring the bad times, but it is accepting them for what they are and learning to grow from them, rather than run away from them. Take one step at a time and try to twist a small bad thing into a good thing- gradually does it.

For example, waking up late AND missing your bus. Rushed off your feet, stricken with panic, how could the day get any worse? Well, the day has only just begun, so don't be done with your day just like that(!) Plus, be thankful for actually having woken up, with running water and food feeling healthy and happy.

The more grateful you are for the little things, the big things become the small things you didn't think were of such importance. Such a simple thing to wake up and feel OK is something we all take for granted. Be thankful for the little things in exchange for breaking out with the compulsion to cling to negative reactions when bad things occur.

Bad things happen to good people, good things happen to bad people. That is the way the world goes; you just have to learn to accept and heal yourself by adopting a more "at least that didn't happen" kind of thought flow…

Radiate and ravish those around you with what you are made of – LOVE. When we can acknowledge that life is ever-changing; we are an ongoing part of that transformation, then acceptance will flow through: it is what it is. Accept what you cannot change, bbu don't get caught up in a cage. Accept, move on and attract positive energy. When confronted with negative talk and sharing it with others, you are only going to bring them down too.

When confronted with negative talk and thinking and share your thoughts with others by seeing the better side to things, they are only going to join in with boosting you because attitudes are infectious; toxic when it comes to a negative attitude. People will steer away from you because nobody wants to be brought down with you - face it, you are part of a world where you have to contribute to thinking things can only get better for things to get better.

Seek out love, kindness and compassion in everything you do.

An abundant amount of influential leaders, religious figures and activists over the years have brought attention to easy remedies, such as stilling the mind and manifesting in a plethora of positive acts in life.

The Dalai Lama says that 'We can shape the future, creating a more peaceful era, by adopting a realistic approach, recognising that the more compassionate you are, the more you'll find inner peace.'

*Picture a tap with negative thoughts running down the drain - cross them out as they disappear when you visualise them.

Yet again, we must meditate upon our thoughts and treat them like water running out the tap, trickling and departing down the sink, not in view any more, with no reason to return.

Visually imagining thoughts like this assists in the practice of meditation, so why not adopt it into everyday life when an undesirable thought arises and you are not comfortable with the way it makes you feel. It can be harmful to attach yourself to thoughts because you are authorising them to become real and have the right to exist. You are subconsciously aware of what you are thinking, seeing and living, especially when teased with fearful feelings.

You are not the thought – the thought is there to scare or prepare. You are the one who is in charge of letting thoughts live on or die out. Sometimes, such damaging thoughts appear out of nowhere, striking suddenly and sending signals of stress to stab at your aura. Your body reacts and is stumbled by the physical pain as well as emotional pain pulling you down. Breathe. Smile. Access a happy thought stored in your mind for a cloudy day like today.

Remember that time, that day or that moment. Override the negative thoughts by accessing happy memories to make you smile and feel grateful or simply see the world with a new pair of eyes each day so you know you can grow. Attack bad thoughts with gratitude.

You can combat the stress through self-love and set yourself free as long as you are aware of the harm that it may cause. For example, you think someone seems to be intimidating, so you suddenly turn offensive. This leads you to take on aggressive feelings that will only disturb your graceful life, so take hold of the thought before you let it live.

The circumstances to follow will be out of control, after participating in the act of negative thinking, because it is easier to be sucked in, rather than slip and slide on the way out.

Catch the thought & let it go.

Count to ten.

Count to twenty.

Take the time to calm down.

We all have the capability of doing so, you just have to believe in yourself. Be confident in taking control. Triumph over your stream of thoughts. Trust me. **Trust in you**.

Look around and light up the world.

A multitude of mannerisms makes people feel uncomfortable. **MANY TIMES** unprovoked by a spoken word because sometimes a look says everything. Have you ever been able to hint at what someone is thinking by just looking into their eyes? It is possible. Our eyes speak into the depths of our soul, so do not abuse the potential power that you can say with your eyes.

Harness your looks for love, light and lure. If you think positive thoughts then you will attract positive outcomes. This is the law of attraction that many might know of and seek out in life. It exemplifies how the universe will serve you according to your mindset.

So if you think negatively, then bad experiences are bound to happen, whereas if you are to think positively, then good experiences are more likely to pursue. It encourages positive thinking as a means to lead a more pleasant and progressive life, where one aims to be cheerful to deter harm and hardship to take over.

If positive thinking is utilised to unite your mind and body, then positive outcomes are the product. When practising positive thinking, the power of the present moment spurs on peace. Peace is energy. **You are at peace.**

Contain this inner energy and it will serve you in crucial times so that you can learn how to support it and reap the benefits of good health and happiness.

If you treat your words with care, then you will treat others with care.

Facing adversity can be a setback, but if you catch the catalyst and concentrate on moving up, then the bigger picture will be the focal point. Focus, be patient. Pushing yourself to put whatever has arisen into perspective, will provoke positive thinking to take centre stage. **Reflect. Rewind. Revise.**

When challenges arise, allow yourself to feel encouraged by setting yourself a goal or visualise yourself in a better situation. Look forward, but stay present. Things do get better in the end, believe it. Hard work pays off in the end, trust in it. Stay confident and cheerful, then you will stay in tune with your inner peace. In any given moment, we can change the way we feel.

Free will is fragile, so are you. We are blessed enough to make our own decisions, so make the best of it and thrive off life. It is up to us to nurture and take care of ourselves so that we can be grateful for the gift of life. We must nurture our thoughts and actions, to reap the benefits of a positive outlook on life.

Once we have discovered the delights in life, then positive thinking will occur more organically, as obstacles become lessons rather than defeats. Flip your focus to see the light, not the night.

Understand how significant and precious free will is. Free will proves that we are in control of how we feel and if we have the choice to feel good, then surely this should be the objective. Make it your objective and find ways that will make you happier, keep you in balance, stray you from arrogance. Shift your attitude to seek out things that make you excited. Feel the drive. The practice of positive thinking reaps boundless benefits in attitude, determination and character.

This way, you will find out that trials and tribulations teach us to be strong and resilient. When you realise that life itself is a lesson, then engagement in learning something out of everything will occur. Intuition is key. Stumbling upon spontaneous situations weighs out worries. Taking on this positive approach will accelerate you further towards a direction of connection and communication.

For example, if you struggle with staying positive, then treat yourself like a flower.

If you don't already have a house plant, then get one! Learn from the way you automatically feed it without any second thinking or hesitation. (I told you, you are made of love!) It is human nature to nurture, but sometimes we forget that we are part of this nurturing process. As you water plants daily, you also need to water yourself with love, care and kindness. Feed yourself with positive people, peaceful places and purifying practices.

Imagine that you are a flower: Feed the flower and it will grow. Water yourself with compliments. Allow yourself to have accomplishments. Praise yourself for those achievements. You can do it if you put your mind to it. Spray yourself with a lovely smell, all ready to go share, and tell. Tell the good news and be aware of what's fake. Feed yourself with positive thoughts and you will grow into a healthy entity. This energy will be absorbed by those around, **attraction forces are louder than any sound.**

Train your brain and take yourself out of the social media mind game

Social media is bonkers. It has this ability to baffle, amaze and infuriate me all at once. For example, the variety of posts may season your day like a spoonful of honey or it may distress your day like a bin bag ready to take out. We are all culprits. For example, I go on Facebook (purely out of boredom) and see awe-inspiring videos of a 100-year-old yoga teacher or a 2-year-old boy who is a genius and just think, wow life is amazing, I am so lucky to be part of such an extraordinarily talented world. Then, two seconds later there is a video of a guy getting the shit kicked out of him and a sea creature dead on the beach due to plastic pollution. My thought stream instantly turns to question, how am I part of such a fucked-up world?

Within such a brief passing of time, our minds are washed with what we see and how we think, making us behave in bizarre but sane reactions.

Our thought process is not only determined by who we surround ourselves with, yet what we see and hear. Understandably so. We have all been given the chance to acquire a voice that 'matters' to a certain extent, where we can post and preach whatever we want, however, we want.

Be it grotesque or glorious, every approach is down to craving attention and seeking a reaction from other people.

It makes sense. So, in such lethargy loaded times, when we are consumed by frivolous scrolling on Facebook, Twitter, Instagram... the lot of them(!), our mind is also consumed, questioned and sometimes conquered by so much to take in.

We turn to judgment and jealousy. Yet, the more you train your brain to be glad to see someone on a deserving holiday or excited for a person to have a new baby, for example, then the more you become in control and content with what you have. Be hopeful when you see a poor boy starving or a sea turtle dying because it will make you more willing to contribute to changing the world.

Adopt an optimistic state of mind that will enable you to take in all the horrors of the world because your light within will show you it is up to us to make a difference, charging you with resilience and will power. Take responsibility. We are our own worst enemy. Look around and realise that we are our own greatest threat. There is hope and it is within us! It is up to us to participate in finding the good news and focussing on how to make things better.

Alternatively (and most commonly these days), Facebook is ridding us of our clear cut consciousness when intentionally negatively interacting with one another and abusing others for the fun of it. If you purely follow pages that plaster negative news everywhere, then you might just be taken down by the rubble of what our capitalist society wants you to do because then you will seek out materialistic and societal ways of escapism to feel OK.

Have a clear out on all your social media. Too much time, right? Yes, I know, but it will be worth it.

Can you even estimate what the average amount of time is that you waste on social media? According to the UK government following a loneliness study due to the epidemic at the minute, people tend to spend an average of 24 hours a week on social media. Startling, that we essentially lose a day of our lives per week devouring social media. What a load of bollocks! (Excuse the language).

We all are guilty of the charge of wasting time on social media because it is how we all stay akin. Such is modern-day life. Media may be destroying you because what you digest daily has a great effect on not only your thoughts but outlook and opinion on life.

Take the time to go through your crowd on social media and make sure that you are following those that interest, intrigue and inspire you. If you feel like some people or news outlets are purely filling your feed with damaging data and you cannot deal with it - unfollow! Easy.

Yes, we should all be aware of the tragedies and turmoil that our world is going through, but sometimes it is best to limit yourself on the downright deterring disclosures that fill up your feed.

Say no. Choose optimism. Keep the faith. Stay positive. The abundant amount of news that flows through daily is too much for our minds to cope with, naturally. If we are accumulated by the sinister ways of the world, then we will feel depressed and sad, naturally. We feel the strain and pain that the world is going through, naturally.

See the positive in everything and you will strive to be a positive person yourself. Suddenly you feel sad after reading a horror story because you are a good person. Otherwise known as empathy. Empathy is important to exhibit in human beings, because if we didn't have it, then change would not occur! We like to blame people. As humans, we do not see ourselves responsible for the mess that we are in, but we are the threat. The modern-day era of climate change and so on (the list is pretty long!) is because of our greed, gain and government…!

Guess what? We are **responsible** and we have to **admit** to it, now more than ever. Once we take responsibility, we can take action. If we know how to digest data in a nurturing nature, then we will know how to take care of ourselves and others around us. It is natural for humans to show empathy, so let us ignite this sunshine state of mind and make a difference with how we like, share, tag and comment on things in the world of wanting to show your "best life".

When reading a post, our thoughts can drift, detain or dote on us. Essentially, our thoughts are the product of seeing something. This is the case with the social media mania, so let us reflect on some simple ways that can make a positive change to how we use our media when socialising.

There are so many stories that spread the joy out there, it is simply up to you to seek and you shall find.

1) Tag to elevate

When someone comes to mind – tag them! Tag someone in something that you see and they come to mind – be it a funny video of a dog eating pizza or a random video of a grandma dancing. Such a small thing can be a big thing! Taking a second to type in someone's name might just elevate their day with fresh energy to carry them through.

2) Like to spread

Like a post of positive news that has made you smile or touch your heart, so it can spread the love that has just been transmitted through the screen into the depths of your soul. The more you like posts, the more viewable they will be for others to look, learn and love from.

3) Share to care

When something has divinely touched you, and you feel the need to share your view – do it. 1) Aim to be thoughtful about what you say because it may be interpreted by others in their way. 2) Accept that we are all individuals with our own opinions and go from there. This way, we are interacting healthily.

4) Comment to encourage

Sometimes you want to comment on something to state your own opinion or to tag a bunch of mates – go for it! If you think that your voice wants to be heard on a topic, then do not hold back, but again, be careful of what you truly want to report. Reflect before you remark, rash comments can be destructive.

We all hold individual opinions about what we want to post and share, but with two simple intentions: to bring others down or lift them. Just as social media has taken over your life, the emotions with it do too. Exchange your energy bring about positive rays of encouraging words, it is infectious and people need sweet little reminders.

Negative thinking can engulf your life within a second, but you can fight it off within a millisecond if a circuit of positivity allows you to see through destruction to see delight. Gratitude is much better than gutlessness upheld by sour intentions. Spread sweetness and stamp out the sourness.

"It is no measure of health to be well adjusted to a profoundly sick society."
— *Jiddu Krishnamurti*

Adjust your expectations... or get rid!

Needless to say, we question everything and expect something. Due to our minds being overtaken by external factors, it is OK to question and expect things, but there has to be a barrier. If we build an internal barrier, then external elements will not matter so much. It is then, that we will realise not all things are the way we want them to be and acceptance will flow through. Expectation and disappointment come hand in hand. Think of them as the evil twin sisters in Cinderella – they cannot work without each other, plus they promote each other's evilness.

No matter how much or little you have depended upon an expectation for a certain amount of happiness, you will always feel a hint of disappointment. Disappointment can send you into a furious, feverish and frenzied state of mind.

SO, how exactly can you control your expectations so that you may have a healthier and happier mindset for positive thoughts to occur naturally? Well, firstly the acknowledgement that expectations are based on one's own belief, dreams or hopes is a starter. You are the creator.

The prospect of something comes from you, even if it is not in your hands to control. Let us take a simple example of food being cooked when you arrive home. Be it a parent, pal or partner, in your mind, this person is going to make you dinner and you expect it to be ready when you get home. By virtue of the prediction planted in your head, you automatically look forward to it (who doesn't want food cooked for them, anyway?!).

You turn up and the turn out is not as expected. No smell greets you with a comforting feeling and no dinner is ready to tuck into. How do you react?

Well, if you depended on the belief dinner was going to be ready, then you would generally feel disappointed. Pretty obvious. So now, the key here is to not let that disappointment take a dramatic effect on your positive thought stream... only attained five minutes ago!

Such a rapid revolution and influx of indications can turn you crazy, but you can take control. Breathe. Remind yourself that disappointment is not life-threatening. Consciously, we are indeed aware of this, however, it is harder at some times to access this mid-tantrum, and that is something I speak from personal experience!

These bad feelings come up because your plan A that was planted in your mind has not happened and plan B seems so far away to reach when it really isn't. Your expected reward of food did not occur, but do not allow it to deter. Dissuade you away from feeling everything is OK – it is not the end of the world. You just have to apply a hopeful state of mind that there is always a plan B or another side to the story. For your mind to take on a positive perspective, you must aim to not have expectations.

It is up to you to be so aware of yourself that not even expectations can pull you out of a positive mindset and down under to disappointment.
When you plant an expectation, you sustain it with hope and gain disappointment. What is the point?

Nobody or nothing can ever fully live up to your expectations, if something that manifests within your mind regularly, but expectations can be exchanged for acceptance where happiness is compelled to follow. Aim for realistic expectations if needs be, rather than based on random seductions on the outside. It is all about stimulating yourself for your worth and not relying on worldly desires, there to downcast your right to reign in inner strength.

Words can mean something or nothing

It's absurd how a word can make you feel on top of the world or like a piece of shit. Words waver there way through to you as quickly as switching a light on. It all depends on your perspective, self-image as well as who is uttering it, of course.

It intrigues and baffles me as to how a compliment can lift me, but if someone who means a lot to me says one word out of line- that is it, I am wound up within an instant. Words say it all. Words can control you, yet they don't mean a thing.

It utterly, completely and depends on how the person receives them. A word can mean a million things or not a single thing at all. It is up to you to decide what you want it to mean and determine how it makes you feel. Think about it. Words are what you are reading right now. You don't have to believe everything I am saying, so why can one word let us believe everything we want it to? Or one word makes us reconsider everything?

Christopher Walken said, "Words are little bombs, and they have a lot of energy inside them." If we visualise words as these bombshells or flower petals, then you truly realise that taking care of what you say is very important.

The effect of a mere morpheme may manage to boost your mood or bring you down. Either way, you are the decision-maker in how the word will affect you or not, even in those split seconds of elation or resignation. The minute you decide to take it as it is and realise that you are in control of how everything and anything makes you feel, things will shift in your favour and the universe will open up to you.

It is all about drive and discipline when it comes to being set in your positive frame of mind. We are the ones that neglect our delicate minds by misleading it to think that we are not good enough.

If we know we are good and tough, then no words are worthy enough to damage or take a hold of us. If you treat your thoughts just like you treat your best friend, then your mind will be bursting with marvellous mood-boosting acknowledgements. Compliment yourself.

Look in the mirror and learn to like what you see. Adore yourself like you are your own idol. Listen to your voice the way you hear your favourite song on replay. Dress to feel cool and confident in your own skin. Treating yourself with care will expand your mind to exert a positive attitude and exercise an optimistic outlook on life.

If you feel good then you will find good thoughts rushing in as the wind does during a rainy day, breezing through the windows and doors bringing a refreshing feeling. It can be that easy. Do not fret, anyone can partake in it, all it takes is practice. Practice positive thinking in simple steps during daily life and you will find that it will come more naturally after a while.

Last Words

Your thinking reflects your character, your persona, your soul. Your thoughts are a reflection of you. So if you focus on your inner energy to prosper in positive thinking, no setbacks will bring you down en route. Stay focussed. Don't let people predetermine your thought process. Take control. Find your flow.

A crucial step in finding your way to positive thinking is not forcing it. May the force go away from you. It can, however, be harder than it sounds, as some people are just not wired in ways to evoke positivity like others are. It's OK.

Scientists have proven that we can alter our brain, through practices such as mindfulness. Two parts of the brain affecting self-control and resilience show that this act of love will enable positive thinking to flow through when practising mindfulness. Since mindfulness is a way to stop the stream of thoughts flooding through and staying still in your presence, it is a brilliant way to start on your path to manifest in positive thoughts. Taking time out – it is crucial in conquering positive thinking.

Become self-sustainable through your stream of thoughts, in a way where nobody can steer your thoughts from your appointed way. When you give yourself this attention to be a better person, positive thinking will be a rippling effect of taking care. All it takes is courage, determination and perseverance to ignite your power of positive thinking.

Write down one thing you love about yourself every day. Then, write something that you love about others in your life. Afterwards, about strangers on the street. Gradually confess to encouraging thoughts about you and those around you, so that you become more grateful and glorious in the path of optimism.

Practice thinking positively, let the negativity quieten down

Overthinking throws you out of your flow, stop it before you feel too low

Stand tall and do not fall, stay sweet to those you meet in the street

Invent rules to stick to, so your optimism will shine through

Take every day one day at a time, start to realise life is sublime

Invite positivity into your life, so you may dismiss the strife

Vengeance is unhealthy, it is for those who are stealthy

Enter into a clear state of mind, begin to find that life can be kind

Doubt

What is doubt?

Doubt is a form of indecision. As human beings, it rises and falls at a sporadic pace that seems to be uncontrollable.

Doubt occurs daily. It unpredictably pops up, out of the blew, into our mind, in an attempt to steer us away from feeling fine.

Doubt can rule us if not taken care of with a spoonful of confidence.

Doubt is dangerous and delirious, it messes with our mind and makes us think of drastic consequences based on no evidence at all, yet still convinces us to believe in its power due to its overriding nature.

Doubt demands our full blown-attention.

Doubt deludes our state of happiness and tinges it with stress-induced feelings so that we feel like failures before even trying.

Doubt drives our thoughts into a whirlwind of contemplations and speculations so that we are trapped in a never-ending cycle of belief and disbelief.

Doubt is a mental state of being stuck between these two propositions. Doubt delights in enticing us with unimaginable situations, so that we become lost and lonely.

Doubt plants the seed of self-doubt into our minds and feeds it with negative connotations of ourselves fuelled by our weaknesses, determined by our diffidence. We get swayed by it, we get sucked in by it, we get lost in it, we get controlled by it.

Doubt rules us. It allows all our negative attributions and thoughts to erupt inside so that we must obsess over them in a hazy state of irrational uncertainty. We come to a standstill of endless speculation, hesitation and hallucination when succumbing to its mightiness.

Doubt is like a devil or dictator in our mind.

Doubt is neither of these though, it is purely something that is in our mind like any other trait, doubt lets the flame. Therefore, it is possible to destroy doubt by developing methods in which we can overcome/exchange a discouraging feeling for an encouraging feeling. Then, we can fight it off with fearlessness and hug it with happiness.

Doubting yourself

As a human being, it is in our nature to doubt ourselves, but we are capable of seeing through it. Detect, overcome and learn from doubt as something to spur your inner strength on. With some acknowledgement and acceptance of where doubt plants itself in preconceptions and preoccupations, you can transform your thoughts into a carefree state of mind. So... Let's start with the basics.

How many times in a day have you doubted yourself? Uncountable, right? Be it from early morning routines like switching off the straighteners or leaving the light switch on, such tiny incidents cause a massive torment in your mind to instantly trigger stress and worry to the point that you must check if something has been left on or if it was all just in your mind (most of the time it is!).

Stop for a moment. When you think about how such a small mishap can have such a dramatic effect on your thought process, it is absurd to accept this regular occurrence of utter madness. See how doubt demands your complete attention to not forget about it until proven right or wrong. Essentially, doubt can take over your life in minor or major ways. Wasting your energy on doubt will cause drought, a drought of self-love so that it can fully take control.

Doubt does not only manage to corrupt our self-judgment skills, but it succeeds in destroying every other thought that is circulating, demanding and taking centre stage.

Doubt demands to be heard, in that way it is like a child. Young children tend to want to be heard and seen, it is pretty normal for a young infant to crave attention. The combination of their curious minds and innocent souls seem to be distant from everything that is happening around them because they simply do not have the capacity to yet know the ways of the world. When giving children attention, we listen carefully and show compassion, then we can react in the right way. So why don't you handle your doubts in the same manner a mother nurtures her child? Simple really: we don't acknowledge doubt as something we can take care of or care for. Take care and take control. Catch it before it overwhelms you. Don't allow the stress to swiftly take hold of your state of mind but see why it is there and where it came from. Who invited it in?

Question it and dominate the doubt before it takes dominion over you, questioning you. With needless distress, one can easily solve them by self-assurance. Reassure yourself that it is OK. Make a mantra like "I can overcome this" or "I know better". Count to three. Take hold of the doubt before it takes hold of you in a hole of helplessness. Settle your mind before it bursts into a frenzy of doubt driven dealings that will drench the mind in a puddle of petty preoccupations. Be it big or small, the doubt has been rooted by something or other, meaning that you can detain, delay and deter whatever it is, away with a positive thought or optimistic approach.

"If you hear a voice within you say, 'you cannot paint', then by all means paint and the voice will be silenced" is a bold statement by Vincent Van Gogh that each one of us can learn from – when you doubt yourself, there is, even more, the reason for you to prove yourself wrong.

We can silence this voice within our mind, all it takes is will power. It is hard, I know, especially when we are surrounded by so many doubt infused publications and programmes in our modern world, making it more toilsome for us to mute this voice that is a vice for media, politics and war to go on.

A little lesson from little ones

We can learn a lot from tiny human beings. They say what they think, they do what they feel like, they are raw pieces of humans that have a lot to give and gain from as adults. Sometimes we are not the "wiser" ones where society has corrupted our spirit. Kids don't particularly give a shit about what other people think. This is one thing we must stand by when dealing with doubt!

Doubt is impressively handled by children at times because they are so driven by a determination that it radically changes their mindset in acquiring a way of thinking where they can achieve anything. If a child can turn doubt into determination, then any adult is capable of doing so.

After all, we were all young once. Just because we are not nippers any more, does not mean that we cannot learn – life is a learning curve itself. This is something we also need to adapt when deterring doubt. Every day we are learning something new without subconsciously realising it. When we learn, we make mistakes. Errors are regarded as a natural part of learning. Therefore, if you have once failed something or have not been able to manage to do something as you had expected, it does not mean that you can't do it now.

Take those experiences as life lessons in how exactly you can make this time different and dissuade doubt by excelling in the mentality that anything is possible if you put your heart and mind to it. You can do anything you want to do. Make it your mantra.

create your mantra here to reflect and relight up your life whenever you feel the doubt drag you down

Fight the fear by feeling more determined than ever, rather than doubtful of anything, something and everything. Be like a child in the way that they fight doubt with determination and show yourself what you are capable of. If you provide doubt with more self-worry and pity to prey on, then it is going to grow in power, but if you supply it with self-care and kindness, then it will soon lose control over your thoughts and life choices.

Stop caring so much about what others think!

The key is to not care. Funny eh?! Also, easier said than done, I know. I say this so much when some of my friends are concerned if they don't think their outfits are on point or if someone will say something about this, that or the other. Who cares? It's a motto that anyone can bring to light. Accept that there is always going to be haters, you just have to shower them with your acceptance, love and kind spirit.

One approach I have endorsed over the years comes from a bizarrely comical little moment after my Opa (grandad in German) took a piss by the side of the road when I was younger. I still remember it now – we were driving, and he needed to go to the toilet, so he simply pulled up and stood by the side of the busy street and did the deal. Straight away in a startled state, didn't you see all those cars go by?!", I asked.

He answered at ease, "Well, I'm not going to see them again, am I?" It astounded me. Then I thought about it. It's so true. Sometimes we care so much about what people think, of whom we don't have the faintest idea about (vice versa). Other times, we care so much about what people think because we want to be seen as bold, bright and beautiful.

My mad and marvellous best friend, Matty, also taught me a lot when it comes to not giving a sh*t. We became best friends during the early days in High School, funnily enough over the fact that we were both being bullied, him for being gay and me for being German. It was pretty funny because it both affected us so much, we would hide away from the haunting shouts at break time.

One day, I remember him saying to me "Who gives a shit? Let them try and bring us down, we are better than that." You see, at our school, we had to walk between campuses and it was then that we would get yelled at. We were always in hysterics because he was hilarious, so we just started to stride with confidence in bursts of laughter with no care of the outside world, because our world was better. He was the funniest person I ever knew, everything he uttered made me laugh out loud. He had the same effect on everyone he met, a jester at heart.

I miss the way he made me laugh so much, but now I look back to think about how lucky I was to have him by my side during the teasing teen times.

We healed our bullying through laughter.

Matty was funny without trying, and it cured our care for these dickheads and turned it into a hilarious state of affairs because they started to realise they weren't affecting us any more in the way they wanted to. From then on, I became less bothered about people's opinions because most of the time it is the bullies that have the issues, so they want to make themselves feel superior by picking on someone else's insecurities.

We all have insecurities, it's just a matter of dealing with them with acceptance and not driving them on with doubt. In the end, I was proud to be German and Matty was proud to be gay. Yet, he never fully accepted him, unfortunately, and passed away. You see, life is about accepting who you are and loving who you become, for doubts and delinquent people to not affect you. Find your people and care about them, that is one way of deterring doubt.

So why is it that we tend to care about what strangers think of us? If anyone, we should care about what the people we love the most think of us, right?

Well… most of us strive to make good impressions, therefore consider people's perceptions to be of utter importance. On the most part, this is not so bad. Normally, we want people to see us in a good light, but the danger lies in concerning ourselves about stranger's views so much that it staggers our views. This can override us from honouring ourselves for who we are and side-tracking us of who WE want to be, rather than who they want us to be. For example, if it gets to the point where you are aiming to please someone else and en route disregard your own feelings, then that's where it goes *tits up*. Nobody can hold you back other than yourself. The drive of doubt these days is heightened through people's perceptions that poison one's reflections, resulting in people to steer away from taking some radical life decisions for themselves. Being so occupied by people's opinions to the point that it controls every element of your life is the worst thing that doubt can do to you.

What does doubt do?

Doubt creeps up when you least expect it or it can linger around like a dirty smell you can't get rid of. One of its favourite times to make an entrance these days is if you are not following the expected societal layout of life. You end up comparing yourself to others, then base decisions on other people's routes of life, eventually losing touch with what you want. This should not be the case.

Doubt drives you to think that everyone is on track. Doubt drives you to look at other people's life decisions. Doubt drives you to think what is expected of you, determined by social norms. There we have it again: expectations. Doubt and expectations come hand in hand because if we didn't have expectations of someone or something, then doubt would not have the right to manifest itself in our decision-making.

You are expected to have a baby. You are expected to do well in your studies. You are expected to have everything planned out. You are expected to get stressed out and take a vacation. You are expected to get a good career and succeed. You are expected to marry and get a mortgage.

These are a few stereotypical societal expectations that seek to sustain themselves through the power of doubt. Just because he or she is flying high in a career, or somebody else has just announced their second baby as well as moving to a new house, does not mean you should do the same. Everyone is different. That is why life is so magical in all its ways and wonders that create our wings to fly in different directions. Do not fret about somebody else's life – accept and be happy for them.

Do not compare yourself and cause unneeded doubt to arise in your mind just because you have decided to do something else or move somewhere else. Flush out the doubt with a yearning to flourish with delight. Extinguish doubt by not caring about people's life decisions so much to the point that it will question your own decisions. Distinguish what your priorities are. Yes, you should care, but you shouldn't compare.

Caring about certain people's opinions may motivate you to make a move or take a step back, it is all about what lesson you are prepared to learn from others by the perspective that you reflect.
There is a difference between caring about other people's opinions so much that they might stop you

from shining to the best of your ability or taking their opinions in an admirable fashion for yourself to flourish from.

So what else can doubt do? Doubt detains us from living our dreams, doubt delays our dreams to come true. The only thing that is powerful enough to deter us from chasing our dreams is self-doubt. This can be triggered by the voice in your mind or even planted by certain people judging you. That voice does not speak the truth.

How do you know if so and so would react in a certain way if you were to do something? The answer is you don't until you have tried it out. You never know anything until you give it a go. Break it down. The voice in your head is spurred on by the doubt of others and the power from within is dulled down by an imaginary state of affairs trying to overwrite your way of staying optimistic. When you practice positive thinking, then doubt is just like an annoying little sister or brother that bothers you now and then.

Yet, you have the authority to push it aside (doubt, that is, not the sibling right now!) and assert yourself in a mighty manner. Picture doubt as something that signals annoyance, so that you can stagger its effect and force its bearing on your mind to be minuscule. To not care about other people's thoughts in driving your decisions, you must be so sure of yourself that nobody's opinion can fucking waver you away from your magic.

May they marvel at you, instead of menace at you because you're doing something for yourself, taking a chance, taking a step forward. Concentrate on what you want to achieve and never let it leave. "I can overcome this." "I am stronger than this." Take these mantras and repeat whenever a hint of doubt appears. Make your mantra and make it something you believe in. Stay focused. Stay secure. Stay one hundred percent sure.

You are worthy and capable of handling your shit without having to worry about other people's pathetic points of view to put you off your powerful prance. Own your thoughts, own who you are.

Instilling doubt in others

We are all culprits of it. At some point or other, everybody has doubted a person they know or a stranger and made it vocally apparent to that person. It's not fair. Right from the start of time, doubt has been a way to side-track someone in their righteous route of self-awareness. Doubt will stumble your way of thinking and send you away from grasping your goodness as well as others.

A good example of the injection of doubt through one another is that of Adam and Eve. Eve instilled doubt into Adam through a forbidden fruit right from the very start, to seek out evil rather than stick to what was known as good. This sort of doubt dismantles our stream of thought to flow like a river and interrupts it with a corruptive wind, producing crashing waves of uncontrollable thoughts, created by someone else.

The river is then raging with force from every direction because we do not know how to escape or where to look. Such doubt is permitted by us to take shape in our thoughts and thereafter actions. This form of doubt can become normalised, especially when being so close to someone else, for example in relationships or close family ties as well as firm friendly connections. Their input in our life is important. We sought to know what our families and friends think about certain things in our life and that is totally normal.

However, when their opinions and thoughts enable doubt to grow and shrink our ability to be self-critical, that is where we must put up a barrier. We should take on their feedback… to a certain extent. If doubt deconstructs our ability to look at our decisions in a way that serves us and not others, then it becomes more challenging to tackle. Self-awareness, self-respect and reflection should rectify the way. Stop and think. Sometimes people's opinions can be a hindrance towards taking decisions because it might feel like they are judging you.

Taking on judgment and criticism, no matter who it is expressed by will sabotage our system of straight thinking if sustained by self-doubt and lack of confidence. Be critical and reflective about yourself, but do not criticise and refrain yourself from saying the last word when it matters the most to you. Contributing is different from control. You must be the master of distinguishing which form of doubt is being promoted in each situation.

In such circumstances, doubt can become debilitating because people who you are closest to can have an extraordinary effect on the way you feel and flourish.

Put it this way, if your loved ones are making you doubt your own decisions regularly, then something is going wrong. You are either making the wrong decisions(!) or they are attempting to restrain your right to know what's best for you. If doubt is fuelled by certain individuals for a long time, it can put you off your path without realising that you are losing control of your life.

You cannot be put down repeatedly without saying something about it, otherwise, it will lower your self-esteem and result in a lack of self-respect, allowing others to make decisions for you. Take back control. Self-affirmation comes first. Strive for self-improvement, but do not let anyone's doubt dissuade you on your way, rather allow it to bring reflection and confidence to light, so your roots may grow stronger. Stand tall. Do not fall. Replace self-doubt with self-acceptance. Self-doubt is synonymous with low self-esteem, so to revive yourself with sureness, you must make a change in how you view doubt catalysed by others as well as by yourself.

    Remember, self-acceptance is a process, so it will take time to overcome the doubts that discourage you away from your inner beauty because doubt could have been occurring for a long time within a relationship, you might not have noticed it or pushed it aside. If this is the case, then realise you must make a choice. If you don't make your own choice, clearly someone is going to make it for you... but it will not be as good as the one you make for yourself. Be the change that you want to be, and you will see!

Unfortunately, people on this planet treat others like shit.

Yet not one single person has the power to make you feel unworthy unless you permit them. Don't let them doubt your bright soul. Stay close to people who make you shine and stray away from those who make you whine. Surround yourself with love and wear it like a glove to protect you from doubt, and learn to be aware of within and without.

Why do major changes make doubt your dictator in decision-making?

We are capable of anything, yet change drives us further away from this affirmation. Most of the time, fear overtakes our power when change interferes. Change is cunning in the way it manipulates our mind to come up with the worst outcomes. Change chases optimism away and pleasantly greets anxiety ridden emotions to enter into our decision-making skills. Sometimes, the prospect of change seems too scary to even consider, so we simply brush it under the carpet, never to come out again... or at least for the time being.

There is no such thing as being ready, mentally, financially, physically, in fact, you are ready when you know taking a chance at life is the only thing we are here for.

Although doubt is essential for intellectual and emotional development, it mostly depends on how we perceive and process it. We must question decisions to determine if they are really what we want to do. We should question decisions made by governments and higher authorities so that we can uphold our right to contribute in a just society. We will question our parent's potency because we want to lead our own lives and be self-sufficient. We could question our professor or doctor because we want our voice to matter when it's something important to us.

There are countless ways where we are accustomed to questioning and doubting, thus doubting is good to practice, but only when we want to spur on a change, not because of a change. It is different when doubt is a motivation for change; it disables us from growing to our full potential. Frequently, growth struggles to rise when change occurs because the "unknown" is what we stumble on in our tracks, inspiring timidity to take over. Fear of the unknown enables doubt to determine our actions, or rather disable our actions from fabricating.

When a major change is deliberated by oneself, then doubt will drive you further away from taking the decision into your own hands and drive you into obstacles that overtake your power. Questions will pop up here, there and everywhere. It will be hard to get rid of them, as they take control of pessimistic thoughts. Don't let them live for long and let them flow away like the waves at the shoreline that come and go. It is like you know what you are 'supposed' to think or do, but doubt fights for its place and fuels our decisions from forming.

Doubt essentially becomes our dictator.

Doubt will then make us come to a standstill, in endless speculation of false lies and pessimistic views, rather than taking a chance and finding out for ourselves what we are capable of (anything if we put our mind to it, I promise!). It makes us feel challenged and churned. It develops a strain on our mind to overthink and discourage ourselves for no valid reason.

If you give the power to doubt, then it will overpower you… think about it. Speak up. Do something. Sit with the feeling of doubt – don't shun it away, but don't follow it through. Instead, question its worth, overpower it with your might that everything will be alright. It takes an open mind to see doubt as doubt and know what the nature of it beholds for you: an intricate state of mixed up feelings that manufacture within our mind and manifest themselves throughout our body.

Doubt can make us feel low, physically and mentally. So many layers of feelings find their way to come alive when doubt is the dictator of decision-making. They are all meticulously intertwined in making you come to this stand still. Movement is essential to destroy the dictator. Knowing your matter is even more essential to destroy the dictator. In this case, doubt can be turned around and enable us to see through it. Question, wonder and investigate why it is manipulating your mind because doubt is born from assumptions and not facts.

If we allow doubt to be our dictator when changes are erupting, then we are ultimately disrespecting our intuition. It will cut us off from opportunities that we consider not worthy of pursuing because it correlates with confiding in our comfort, rather than connecting with our purpose. It is harder to connect with passions and purpose when doubt is lurking around, pushing trust aside to remain in the distance.

Be the change you want to be. Be the change you want to see. If you give yourself permission to reflectively look at doubt, then everything will be okay. Write your pros and cons out, so you can visually perceive your doubt posted on paper. If writing lists isn't for you, then think about why this change is making you feel fear and doubt. Meditate on it. Breathe in and out. Take a shower. Take a walk. Take time. We are constantly changing, so doubt can cause distress, it's bound to happen. Every day is different, so start to feel determined by the presence of doubt and not discouraged.

There will be added strains that bring up past experiences, causing you to compare, for example. No day is the same, so your past does not always determine your future. Permit yourself to criticise but don't doubt. Practice critical thinking to spur on self-development, this way you will exceed your expectations and not limit yourself to assumptions.

Free yourself from doubt

In life as we know today; fast-paced, disruptive and technology-obsessed, it is easy to be actively focussed on acquiring things that everyone else seeks out – fortune, status, success, security, and to then show off about it. We think that these are the things that lead to true happiness, but instead, bring doubt and fear to triumph in our mind space. The key to happiness is simply to let go and be free of worldly restraints so that we can truly appreciate the greater things in life. Just as happiness is a choice, so is letting go of doubt and demotivating feelings alongside that further you away from realising your true potential.

As mentioned, doubt is not always unreasonable. It repeatedly keeps us from trying or making things real and attempts to rule over us. However, it can become an insight into what we want, a reflection that we can cultivate for acceptance. An unconditional acceptance of self-worth rather than self-doubt. Look at the good in yourself and others; try to understand and accept each person for who they are, then there will be a certain sense of connection and collaboration, rather than control and cowardliness.

Doubt can show us what we are capable of and is essential in our self-development. It is healthy to question things when a change has to happen, but do not doubt yourself when change occurs in life, rather learn to trust yourself. Tackle doubt by noting how you respond immediately to situations before doubt has its time to disorderly divulge into your decision-making skills. Allow it to unravel the underlying truths deep within, so you may grow in wisdom.

Beginning something new always involves some degree of the doubt to intervene, which is quite debilitating, but normal. If you yearn to have a sense of openness to endless opportunities, then your perspective will change and you can use doubt to source out what feels right in life as well as what you truly want.

Doubt will always sneak up at some point in your life, no matter what. It is bound to happen, but you do not have to bound yourself to it, that is the difference. You get a great job and you question it. You meet someone amazing, but you still wonder "Is this it". You are invited to a wedding and you question what, when and how yours will be. You are out with the people you love and feel the most comfortable around, yet you still seem to question if and how you belong.

Great things happen, and you still ask why. Accept blessings for what they are and accept yourself for who you are, then doubt cannot determine your trail of thought nor tinge your feeling of ecstasy. Stop wasting your energy on questioning and doubting, rather, start sharing your energy in trusting and believing.

Drought the doubt out

Who cares what people think?
It's only gonna make you sink.
Deep down into the doubt,
Look up and peer right out.
Arm yourself with a heart of stout
(not the beer, just to be clear!)
Get to know yourself inside out
And give yourself the benefit of the doubt
Don't worry, you will figure it out
Just simply keep an eye out.
You are your missing link,
So, get with it and stay in sync.

Fear

What does fear mean?

Fear is a cunning, crafty condition of the mind.

Fear finds its way to motivate us, but fear also finds its place in making us feel uncertain, succeeding in shackling us to chains of misery or chains of mystery.

Fear grapples with our emotions. Fear feeds off of our failures.

Fear is the product of the unknown.

Fear drives us, fear fuels us, fear fuels wars all around us.

Fear has a force for humongous harm or the greater good.

It harvests itself inside our dark doubts about ourselves to gain its glorious control over our lives in certain circumstances.

Fear fantasizes on the fact that humans are far from perfect.

Fear is like a lion, the way the courageous creature is always ready to pounce on its prey mirrors how fear fights our confidence when strength is needed.

Fear takes over our body and mind with a storm of stress-induced spirits. Fear stuffs us full of crippling emotions that can dismantle our stability and strength.

Fear feeds at our fidelity of the outer world so that we cannot focus inwards.

It torments our lives from an early age through its ability to dictate our decision-making in myriad methods right up until our ultimate years of life.

As a child, fear comes in the form of a film, a

teacher or a nightmare. We get to know the feeling from a young age and are taught to ignore it rather than identify the root cause, take hold of it and release it. As an adolescent, we are afflicted with fear to follow the right crowd, make good choices and do well in our studies.

During these years, fear becomes a friend and a foe so we can stay in the know. Fear makes regular visits throughout our pubescent years, perplexing the mind about who we are, why we are here and how we should feel. Fear follows us through adult life, prodding and probing at our governing of life and nudging us to follow societal expectations. It may make us feel fragile and feeble in its ability to manipulate our train of thoughts.

It may also be beneficial to assist in completing tasks or to conduct ourselves correctly. It is the way we can conquer the fear that will allow us to flourish from it, instead of hiding away from reaching our full potential. This entails the endorsement of a mindset that encourages an open and optimistic approach of life, ready to release negativity and nightmares with an essential quality to fully focus on the now. This is how to defeat the function of fear in everyday life.

What is fear for you? List words in storm clouds on the opposite page.

Fear follows us for a lifetime… if we let it

Fear appears at different stages in our lives, bewildering us by its presence and purpose. As a kid, fear consists of losing your mum in the supermarket or missing out on a birthday party for misbehaving. Fear is simple (although it seemed like your life was ending back then!), or at least in our adult knowingness of fear because they are unaware of the bigger picture and are not yet conscious or led on by worldly fears.

As a teenager, fear takes on the form of being a cool kid. If you aren't considered fun or interesting, then it is the end of the world. Simple as. Fear kicks in when you want to be acknowledged and accepted into a crowd, no matter what age you are. As a young adult, fear becomes a reality through finding a job or a spouse, prompting the effect of disorientation. Furthermore, the fear is spurred on by exams and passing with a good grade, which is bound to happen numerous times when being a part of the education system. Either way, fear is injected into us like a flu jab that fights off our natural frame of mind for a rightful place, resulting in us feeling inferior and insecure.

Fear takes time to drive away

Adulthood hit me like a car and I admit it was something I seemed to struggle with when it came to the persistent fear that arose with responsibilities, choices and appearance. Fear was always lurking around me like a nasty smell; hard to get rid of as it took a hold of who I am. Questions arose as I wondered what my place was in the world – everyone had ambitions and goals to achieve, but sometimes I just felt like I was drifting in my daydreams.

When my best friend suddenly passed away at the age of 21, I felt like I had failed him, but the previous, persistent fear I daily experienced on behalf of him had suddenly vanished. I had given my all in trying to help my dear and closest friend to find his way. The fear had gone because I had finally realised that it was not my responsibility and I could not have shown him his way by purely being my positive self, because it was up to him to find out for himself. After that, I practised more yoga and prayed more because this ritual made me feel so much better and connected to myself.

I appreciated the time to myself more than I ever had before. The more time I took out to remind myself everything is OK, the finer I felt. Reminding myself of all the things I am grateful for, including my life, was remarkable. It allowed my perspective to widen, authorise myself to feel OK and seek out goodness and gratitude in everything I did. I discovered how I could deal with fear by focussing inward and taking my time to figure out what I want to do and reflect on who I want to be by coming to stillness.

This is the problem- it is too easy to be taken away by the impact of society's pressures in shaping our character to fit its boundaries, but not ours. Remind yourself of how good it is to grow and give. The fear fights for its place during adult life, like a baby craves its mother's embrace. Worrying about my best friend had shown me exactly this. Fear loves being present. It's like your cat or dog who is always there, desiring attention. It will only fester within when you give it that attention!

There is a constant fear in us all about the ones we love. That is because we are human and we care. Fear takes on the form of concern. Fear always makes an appearance. As a parent or partner, you seem to be filled with fear for your loved ones' security and contentment. That means love. When you love someone, fear is healthy because it shows you that you care.

Fear finds its way to obscure your vision of the world by doubting certain people and decisions, never letting you go as it sustains your worries and wiggles in for first place. Then as an elder, the fear of loneliness may stick around and be upheld by the fear of imminent death dawning in.

All in all, fear is ever-present throughout our course of existence and it can come like a tsunami, gaining its glory through the unknown or sit by your side to snatch away any glimpse of gladness by asking "what if..." followed by a dreadful thing. Fear chokes and churns your tummy into knots, testing your patience, questioning your existence. "What if this?" or "what if that?". Fear is a fad. If we let it live, then it will follow us through to our death bed, but if we see it as a thought that can be destroyed, it can be defeated with bravery and a right to be raring in life.

I got the power – you got the power – we all have the power! What power? The power to regain the glory that fear fights us for our whole life. Fear is a feeling that you let live within and without you. Fear is a trick of the mind. We have more strength than we think, and neuroscience is evermore proving that fear is easier to overcome than we assume. Thus, fear can be deplored by building blocks of confidence and care over the condition that we can indeed control.

Let us explore the simple steps to overcome fear by putting trust in ourselves.

How to overcome fear?

Firstly, fear arises in an array of forms. It may occur momentarily when we are confronted with something that scares us or it might be planted within us from an experience that does not wish to leave us. All in all, fear arrives on our doorstep with visitors tagging along that act like a virus towards our perspective and personality, penalising our positive outlook, clasping on to our weaknesses. It can take over as a natural disaster, sucking up every crumb of confidence and replacing it with feelings of doubt, depression and desolation. Like any other disaster, it may strike suddenly with no warning, evoking a major feeling of inferiority.

Fear is natural. The real rational type of fear relates to the certain predicament we find ourselves in. Let us take one of the worst killers of our time: cancer. Along with cancer comes the extreme case of fear as it floods the gates of stability, destroying its outer shell, leaving a naked and vulnerable state. Through this battle to live, there are always heroic stories showing us how fear has been won over because of the love that lives on. Lesson 1: heal fear with love.

Love is endless and every one of us can love like there is no tomorrow. We ache for love when we *are* love. In challenging times, our perspective matures and allows us to prioritise the present moment and forget about the fear that once overwhelmed us. (That is why I took cancer as an example as it sparks the fear of death). When shown love, admiration and care, the empty feeling that fear sinks itself into is instead filled up with the magic of kindness and consideration.

If these attributes are not acknowledged, then it is easy to sink low and let fear drown us. Fear may feel like it can defeat us... Fear can defeat us. It can destroy us if numb and not ready to reflect on feelings.

To overcome fear, you must face your feelings. Own them. Own your emotions to the extent that nobody can partake in the handling of them. Taking such an extreme case of cancer can be a life lesson for us all, even if we are not directly affected. Such a dreadful diagnosis should not be inflicted upon the number of people that suffer from it. However, like any other critical condition or circumstance that we face, it allows us to see the bigger picture. Putting things into perspective definitely determines a sense of overcoming, where one can conquer fear with courage and complacency. Lesson 2: Acceptance of the fear is key.

Develop techniques to tackle your fear. When managing your feelings, you will set yourself free on the journey of wandering within.

First, understand what it is. Second, figure it out for yourself. Thirdly, grasp your competency to defeat it before it takes hold of you. Fourth, reorient your mindset to shift from fear as a contemplative thought and not as an actual thing that can control you but rather take control - you are the commander. Fifth, question the fear's ability to live and exchange the pain for gain. Sixth, gain confidence from your fear and conquer it with a smile. Write a list now of all the fears that you have, from small things such as spiders to bigger things like bungee jumping in clouds and cross them out.

Physical fears vs. emotional fears

Focussing in on the physical fear, to begin with, will enable the emotional fears to come into focus. Physical fears are spurred on through our sensory reactions, meaning the source of fear is dependent on touching or seeing something. Physical formulas of fear provoke the way we look at things based on our preconception of the outside world mostly. A natural state of consciousness reached through meditation is seen by the Dalai Lama as letting go of these fears that are induced by future plans, anticipations and hopes.

Displace yourself with such fears and it will allow you to overcome them.

Let's take arachnophobia – one of the most common and oldest phobias, according to research. Yup, that old cobweb (haha I had to) the fear of spiders. Spiders seem scary to many, so much so it could be considered as a global perspective, driven by the people, heightened by a collective and somehow embedded into our minds to make us feel a certain way... fearful of the nasty buggers! We are all told how to perceive and react to certain things, locking us in a frame of mind, so we can't figure it out for ourselves. Become consciously aware of these fears that are fed to you and fight it off with the energy that you want to emit.

Focussing inwards allows you to know the essence of the fear and most important question it. Questioning things spurs one's mind to engage in unforeseen emotions and bring them to light. Ask why and fly high. Ask why and stop the lies. The lies that persist in prioritising the feeling of fear to demand attention and take over emotions. If you acknowledge that you are capable of controlling the fear because it is based on your reaction or expectation, then you can learn to react differently.

Lesson 3: React in another way.

Take a look at your list from before (if not written, think about it in your mind!)- do they have a connection other than the fact that they frighten you!? Is there something that strings them altogether? How can you overcome them? Gaining clarity about your fears is a fabulous way to work out where your fear stems from deep within. A lot of the time, acting out in wicked ways stems from a lack of love, for example. Simply writing this list is a step closer in conquering your fears. You are accepting and admitting to your fears by writing them down and further acknowledging them in their purest state.

   Normally, when we are frightened of something, we escape it by ignoring the root cause and aim to forget about it. We don't feel fit to beat the fear. To treat any infection, it is necessary to find a remedy. Adopting this attitude to your own emotions is essential to facilitate the feeling of connection and security with oneself. This is why the fear of emotions is a common fear that plenty of people suffer from. Processing emotions is tough, but it is better than burying them deep down because it will, by all odds, come up later on. It can be difficult, but it is manageable. Take note of ways to overcome these fears by setting yourself little goals. For example, there is no better way to overcome the fear of heights other than to confront it by putting yourself up for the challenge.

   This way, you will prove yourself wrong and gain clarity, confidence and contentment when completing something that you never thought fit for. Facing fear exposes yourself to what is and what was and realising what is now can be the answer to everything. Distinguish the fine line between choice and condition.

OK, one step at a time. Solely writing the list won't beat all your fears, yet it will make your mind alert, bringing them to the forefront of your subconscious, so that if a fury of fear is to emerge in your mind, you will be aware of it. In this moment of total acceptance, you can confront the fear by overcoming it or allowing it to take hold of you. It is up to you. You have the choice to confront your fears or stash them away for another day. Fears lurk around us like a crying child who will not cease to give in until cradled by its mother.

The medicine to manage fear is to manifest in your own individual beauty by believing in yourself.

Believe in yourself more than you believe in the fear, whatever it might be.

Mental or emotional fear is one of the most powerful emotions embedded within our deepest secrets and darkest pains. Anxiety, stress, depression are forms of fear regularly raiding our cabinet of self-control, in our delicate minds. Such sorts of fear spiral out of control, taking over our lives at points and paralysing us from choosing joy over misery. It tampers with our mood and takes us to the edge, even to the tip of death, driving us far away from our true selves. Emotional fear holds us back in doing things we want to do because we are unable to shift our perspective due to the dominance held over our mindset, made through clinging on to our most dreadful disturbances. They trap us in the darkness... and don't let us see the daylight. The control of such fear is a cycle hard to break, but it can be done.

Have no fear to face your fear. A lot of the time fear causes us to react in a frantic physical panic. By coming to stillness and controlling the breath, anything is possible. Breathe in and breathe out. Admit to the physical feeling as it takes over your body, feel the fear intensify, taking over certain sensations as it tightens your chest and shivers through your body. This may be called meditation, where the main focus is actually to defocus and not force anything other than recognition to occur. By allowing emotions to pass by, you can process and overcome what is holding you down.

Many people manage fear and all the toxic moods instilled in us through meditation. Once your list has been written, be wary of what frightens you. Take the time to meditate upon the feeling that it causes and utilise your breath to let go.

Visualisation aids in fighting fear.

What I do: Visualise each fear as a cloud drifting by- you can see it and you are aware of it – but you do not interrupt it – you are an onlooker— it goes by – let out a big sigh – now breathe and be still – that is where you have the will – the will to be present – the will to be where you are – the will to be just as you are with no added extras.

How fear holds us back:

Just as doubt delivers demotivation in our will to live a life full of happiness, fear does too. Firstly, fear of the past crawls around our mind (although it is done and dusted!) and induces the fear of the future to occur. Usually, when apprehensive about our future, our previous past decisions come in to play because we do not want them to happen again. It is normal to be critical of not making the wrong decision… again and again. However, it is impossible to live the same experience. Remember this. Experiences can be similar, but never the same. We can never live the same moment nor revive the same feeling, we can only remember the way it made us feel. Although we are aware of this, it still seems to hold us back in making life decisions because the fear is still alive, lurking within and not wanting to let go.

The fact we cannot relive anything more than once could be seen as a positive and a negative. Let's see how:

See the positive:

1) It is undeniably unique and extraordinary that every moment is special in its own magical way. No moment will ever be the same again. We are ever-changing and flourishing as each day passes by and this should be seen as something glorious because we get a new opportunity to learn and grow from every day's delights and dramas that appear in daily occurrences. Look back. Reminisce.

Pleasantly ponder, but aim to be present. Fill yourself with luck, joy and gratitude for having had the chance to experience everything for what it is and how it has made you who you are right now. Accept what you cannot change and smile. Feel glad to gain an appreciation for every moment that passes by and accept them for what they are.

This way, every fleeting moment may be seen as a blessing in some way or other because you view them all as life lessons. Take something from everything. Everything can mean something. You are never in the wrong place, you are not "supposed" to be somewhere else and you are put in a place for a reason. You are the decider of your life! You are here and you were there, that is the wonder of life. Learn, live and love. Learn from each hour of the day, live fully in every moment, and fall in love with life.

See the negative:

2) It sucks that we can never rewind to the "good old days" or a specific time that could be viewed as better than the one right now, and that is exactly where we go wrong. Comparing. Sulking. Nothing betters times like these, it only worsens them. Wishing for something that can never come true, no matter how hard you wish. If you empower yourself to appreciate and accept every moment for what it is then it will not be so hard to stay humble. It is however hard when we feel like we are stuck sometimes and just simply want to go back to when things were better, I get it.

A verse in the bible sweetly summarises this feeling of which I remind myself in such times of reminiscent nostalgia: "Do not say, "Why were the old days better than these?" For it is not wise to ask such questions. Wisdom, like an inheritance, is a good thing and benefits those who see the sun."(Ecclesiastes 7: 10-11).

In other words, it is not wise to long for past times nor ask such questions because it takes your mentality to a moment that has already taken place. This wistful way of thinking entails living in the past and not embodying the present moment. We are wise when we watch the sun come up every day and be glad for another day of innovation.

There is always a positive and negative in every circumstance in life. That is just the way it is. Yin and Yang, this and that. It is up to you to weigh them out in your way. Balance plays a pivotal role, as well as taking everything as it comes, for what it is. Aim to balance the negative with the positive. Weigh them out so that you can live a fair and fine life following your path of progression and not regression.

Why we fear failure before even failing.

Each one of us has not followed something through because the fear of failure has prevented us from progressing further with the idea. We fear failure before even failing and in the process end up delaying our decisions to fabricate. Where is the sense in that? This makes us fizzle with defeat rather than sizzle with delight, bearing a prosperous perspective before even beginning. What are we actually defeated by, though? Our mindset. It all starts and stops in your mind. What you provide power to, will have power over you. So if you let the fear of failure dominate over you, then nothing will get done.

Change your attitude – it is that easy. There have been a plethora of studies showing that success transpires from the kind of mindset we aim to attain: either fixed or growth.

According to a psychologist who dedicated her career to researching attitude and performance, Carol Dweck:

"Failure is information—we label it failure, but it's more like, 'This didn't work, and I'm a problem solver, so I'll try something else.'"

It has nothing to do with who is braver or cleverer, it has to do with how we view things and how being resilient is a chosen frame of mind, just as being resistant is. It is due to the fact that we have gotten into this sceptic state of constantly labelling everything these days, where our system spurs us on to do so by pretty much sorting us all in to "classes" like we are in a game of monopoly (which, in my opinion, is just bullshit in its finest form so that we can be controlled quite adequately by governmental bodies).

Each one of us can be whoever we want to be. OK, if one is from a richer background, then there might be a higher chance of succeeding and being financially stable than a broke person because the funding is readily available, but it is not necessarily always the case. The more money we have does not mean the wealthier we are as a person.

Failure is not based on how much money we have in the bank – the fear of failure is what makes us human. It has nothing to do with class, background, race or any of that shit; you can be who you want to be, so don't let anyone make you think less. It is about your mentality and making the most of opening up to the world with a candid display of readiness to roam, rave and ride your wave. Your mindset is mandatory in conquering the fear of failing.

People with growth mindsets are ready to take action because they focus their energy in finding a positive out of a negative and know that failure can only be a debilitating emotion if you enable it to take control of you. There is never a moment that is "right".

If you are waiting for that moment to arise out of thin air, then sorry to say, but it won't happen. If you are fixed in your ways, then you are bound to avoid something before starting it because the fluctuating feeling of fear overwhelms you and scares you off. You assume you cannot take it on, so you simply avoid it. If an open mindset is approached, limits do not exist because fear is something that spurs you on, rather than paralyses your effort to even take place. Instead, fear is taken off the stove to simmer and cooled down by a chilled sense of handling the matter – process it to improve.

The power to believe that we can perceive, process and persist on with any sort of nervy emotion is the key to be free of fear.

Oprah Winfrey asserts: "There is no such thing as failure. Failure is life trying to move us in another direction."

When we figure out that failure is purely an obstacle in our path, then we find failure as an opportunity to flourish and bloom. Turn that fantasy into reality. These days it is harder to grasp and gain from, but if you aim to not be frightened of the fear that holds you back, then you can scrap it with a confidently sharp smile and stance.

One of the most effective ways is to be mindful in everything you do. These days, mindfulness is managing a lot of people's stress-related emotions and more and more people are embracing the act of self-love due to the strenuous schedules and time-limited lives we end up being put in to by the system. Look around you. Smell, see, feel and breathe. How does it feel to be alive and take everything in around you? Being mindful purely means being alive and making the most of what you perceive to ensure you believe... in life, love and most importantly *YOU*.

Take time out. This can be one of the most effective ways in which you will battle fear. Find your way to combat fear. Read. Garden. Recycle. Cook. Clean. MOVE ON. There is a superfluity of styles to treat yourself well and take the fear out of the equation! Fear teaches us many lessons, most of all it teaches us acceptance. Accept who you are, accept where you are, then you will go far. It spurs us on to be strong and shine our light when we feel we don't have sight.

Let it show you your light within and wonder about what the fear is gaining – nothing.

Stop being frightened to BE you—be fearless in who you are.

Remember: your competition isn't anyone but yourself.

Your competition is you:
Your laziness.
Your haziness.
Your craziness.
Your niceness.
Your eagerness.
Your diet.
Your ego.

The knowledge you neglect as an effect.
The negative behaviour you foster and nurture.
Give it the heave-ho and let go.
The bad thoughts you encourage in your head as you overthink.
Your lack of creativity and energy that makes you sink.
Compete against you and make sure to stay true.
You will get through, just be cautious of feeling blue.
Manage your weird feelings with meditation, mindfulness and the magic that lies within you.

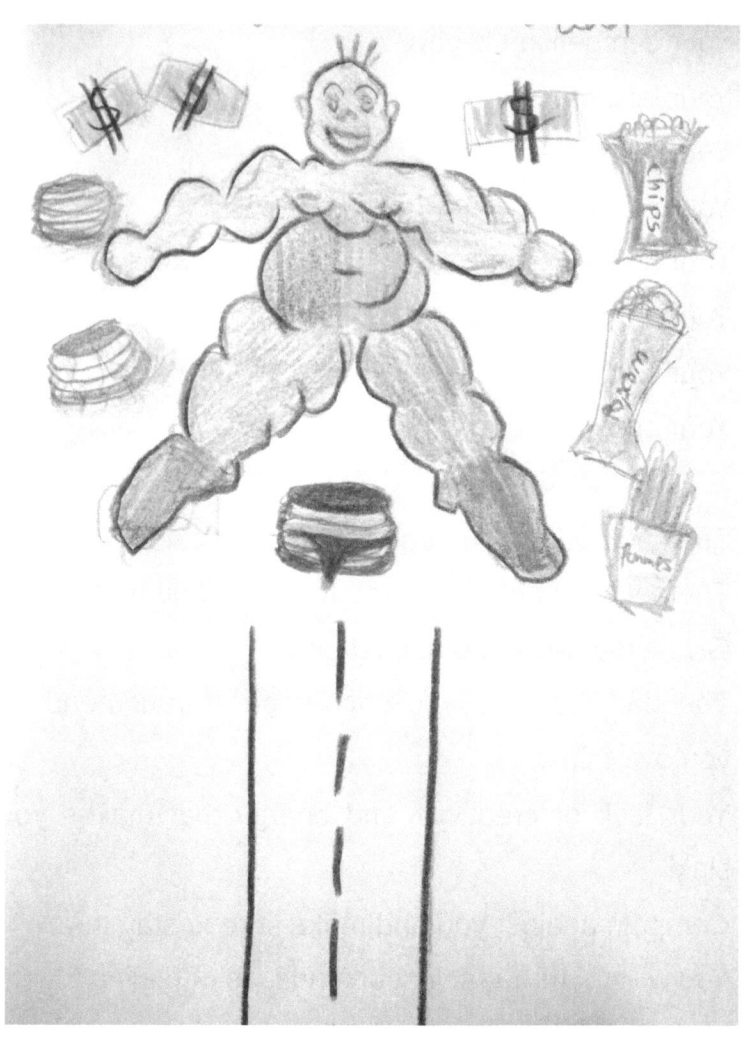

Greed

What is greed?

Greed gets to us all. It is a disorder driven by society, stirred up with the two main ingredients of desire and dissatisfaction, both disregarding our positive outlook as well as valuable intentions and turning them into selfishness. It is cultivated mainly through our culture of consumerism and manipulation of materialism, effectively managing our greedy actions.

It is clear to say that we are all currently in a state of suffering and self-depreciation. It is even truer to say that greed has a great part in this making. Greed means gaining more on the outside but not within. Gaining more materialistic items, for example, entails a constant craving for the next better thing. Materialism is man's worst enemy when it concerns cupidity.

We are forced to want a lot and begged to give

something back. The more we consume, the less inclined we are to contribute. Greed causes one to take, yet not take heed. We are shadowed by social media, showered by its judgment and influenced to feel inadequate pretty much every time we take a look at our screens. Thus, making it not entirely our fault to be roped into acting out greedy tendencies. The western world installs this persistent need for instant success and happiness in us all, based on one of the seven personality traits and deadly sins that attempts to sustain a flame in us all: greed. How?

We are misled by marketing schemes as a means of false fulfilment and temporary satisfaction, submitting ourselves into a never-ending cycle of wishing for what we don't have and wanting what we don't need.

So that we can put our guard up against greed, we must distinguish exactly what dangers are involved in driving our greed to take centre stage in life, by being wealthy in ways that do not serve our soul (and so on in our current state of affairs.)

In its simplest form, greed is the condition of wanting more than you require.

In essence, it is an impulsive state that is sold to us by society.

In theory, it is one of our seven dark flaws that feeds off fear and fright. In general, greed entertains a compulsive need to want more than we already have, based on our insecure state of self and surroundings.

When greed means seeking out material items, it can only deliver short-term satisfaction. Simple as. It wears off and regains power by the curse called money, making cupidity a kind of addiction. We are spurred on through society's capitalism, corruption and concentration of control to cunningly lie to us that money buys everything. We run off greed. Greed is the goal.

Greed makes us roll, yet greed makes us pay a heavy toll deep down within our sad soul. Through greed, we have the compulsion to consume more and care less about what is real and around us. Rather, we care more about the worthless shit and in the process, lose grasp on what truly matters the most. Do our possessions and ambitions win over our family and friends? It seems to be the case these days...

We focus on the material world or business industry, taking us to a certain point of practical possession, momentary strikes of success, yet nothing much more. Being in powerful positions privileges us, possessing things gives us power, but being empowered is a whole different drive.

At the end of it all, the question that matters the most is: Can it be true that the more we own awards a remedy for our unhappiness?

No, it seems to be the other way round; once we have boarded the train of relentlessly requiring more, the harder it is to disembark the darkness that takes us further away from our true frame of mind, nature and feelings. Let's board the train and see where it takes us to view the potential of progressing further in life without greed tripping you up en route.

Greed in daily life

Greed spreads like fire in our senses when we see something we want and roars with zeal as we feel like we will be happier if we have it. It is caught like a disease in the way that it makes us feel weak at our knees. It is difficult to resist but easy to follow because it feeds off compulsion, compelling us to become addicted to an epidemic our modern world pushes us towards more and more through accurate advertising and meticulous marketing. Greed is easier to acclimatise to in life because of the way that our society steers its strength in surrounding us with success through working, earning and buying more.

Generally speaking, greed within our society is the stigma that succeeds in making us feel less than what we are, where the focus is to better ourselves on the outside for all to see and not on the inside to simply be.

Be content with who you are, be OK with what you've got.
Being is more than having, being you is more than anything.
Be delighted by daily occurrences, naturally awaiting your look and love.
Direct your energy into the universe, then you'll see things could always be worse.

The only way in which we can rid ourselves of greed is to identify with something beyond materialistic matters and outward beauty... Honour yourself to the extent that you can realise that greed is just a condition that will bring you down and not bring out the best.

Focus on the things that will increase your mood, heighten your spirits and show you you are more than what the materialistic world has on offer. Our man-made atmosphere can only reach a certain point of practical happiness within us. What is paramount for our battery to stay charged are internal factors such as compassion, consciousness, awareness… the list goes on! These are the things that thrive to determine our long-term fulfilment through connecting to ourselves and letting ourselves be.

Moreover, these are the things that guide one in finding peace, joy and love in everyday life. With open eyes and a pure heart, you will be able to see things for what they truly are and not attach yourself to the outer desires of the world in which we are all entangled in at some point of our lives.

The word expectation arises in this equation of letting go of greed. It addresses the same challenges we face when releasing expectations. The expectation here relies on the notion that greed is a prevalent and present feature in our world, making it harder to rebuke or dispute. It is limitless in its power as people yearn to have more money to feel a sense of security and satisfaction.

Indeed, you may feel chuffed after purchasing something, be it the latest technological device (whatever it is!) or having a fine dine experience, but this feeling fades over time. Whereas, mindfully spending money on travelling, events spent with loved ones or donating to a charity will make you much more felicitous, filling your heart with warmth at the same time as spending.

Greed takes over when thinking about the next thing you may be interested in having your hands on. As a result, greed only lets you take and not give. This places critical tension upon our characteristics, goals and wishes because such a sour sort of trait is not attractive and will trap you in a world where you are so absorbed by the greed that it eventually becomes your sole determination... and destruction.

The expectation of feeling fulfilled from greedy aspirations will never be enough because these expectations always entail endless amounts of reliance on a future feeling, so disappointment is sure to stand in the doorway, banning you from taking a step further. When expectancy exceeds us, the ride of greedy desires does not stop, unless you become aware of actually how unrewarding all the man-made stuff is.

Hence, it only takes a change of perspective and humble heart to rid yourself of greed and turn it into generosity.

That is the best thing to do: switch from selfishly taking to unselfishly giving.

Sharing is caring

Exchange putting your energy from the covetousness consummation into a hunger to heal yourself and others by acclimating to genuine motives of kindness, curiosity and keenness. Buy less, be more. One of the main ingredients in a long life is to share, which in turn is the opposite of greed. The more you give, the more you receive.

The grandness of benevolence takes on a major role in so many religions and moral values because it boosts us to become better people, by manifesting in each other's enchanting auras, bringing out the best in one another. Be love, bring love, share the love.

Choosing to gage your spirit into positive and more rewarding sentiments like generosity instead of greed can provide you with yields of love and light.

The simple act of giving concerns love, whereas greed involves harnessing hints of hatred and hunger for something that will not help others nor yourself. So what's the point? Rather than a win-win with generosity, you lose the love that is lurking around waiting to be harnessed for the good of the world. Generosity is one of the most profound and precious things we can perform as humans, so that we may heal and participate in something so much bigger and beautiful- the greater good of the people. However, it is harder to grasp since we have lost touch with ourselves in this torn up money-driven world of ours.

So much so, we have chosen avarice over service purely because it is the easier option of conforming to society's pressures and modern-day meddling with our mind.

Yield in love, choose love. Love conquers all, remember?

Working with children has shown me how naturally giving little human beings are. We are wired to be kind. Believe it or not, but it is the case. At break time, the children bring a multitude of snacks from home. Some have a sandwich, others have chocolate or even a piece of fruit! I love watching them curiously study each other's snacks sending them into a state of intrigue
(not jealousy).

They will then ask straight-up "Can I have some or exchange you a piece for this?" if not already shared without a second thought. Fancy that- learning such a basic notion from children can open up our eyes to kindness at its finest.

So why am I mentioning this? Well, we can learn from little one's conduct and unfoldings, yet untouched by our self-serving society. Don't hesitate to offer a homeless person the extra croissant you bought because it was on the reduction section. Think about another person who is less fortunate than you, buy one get one free could make someone oh, so happy. Just smile at people, you don't have to go out your way.

Tell someone you like their hat, it could make someone's day. Do something without expecting something back, be real and do the deal. Don't stop yourself from asking someone to swap something with them because you think they would suit it better than you. Don't let yourself be suspicious straight away, rather acquire a curiosity for the little things and let that help you thrive in kindness and compassion.

Giving is an essential quality that should be exemplified on a day to day basis between one another because it provides a positive power, relieving us of the mess made by mankind. Something so special and sincere about the act of giving is that it works both ways. In other words, the receiver does not feel "obliged" to give back, but rather, it is a momentary sensation in sync with our true feelings, instigated from within our heart.

Sometimes, when a kind gesture is acted out as a kind of "instinct" behaviour, our typical response would be to deny or wave off such a saintly deed. We feel unworthy almost instantly. When accepting the offering, we are bound to exhibit some sort of wish to return the love that has been expressed. Generosity, therefore, guarantees a genuine bond to be formed between people, incomparable to anything else, where we then pursue to foster a better version of ourselves with others in mind. It comes naturally.

Through giving, an abundance of energy is created where we can prosper in positive reciprocity with people around us. Through being kind, we discover how to give freely and love limitlessly.

As Churchill wisely stated, "We make a living by what we get. We make a life by what we give." When you give you feel good. It has been widely acknowledged that we gain more gratification and a sense of satisfaction when sharing rather than holding back.

Giving is something so simple and significant- it is one of the first things we are taught from an early age, so how is it possible to lose such a link to vitality and vigour as we grow up? The answer is also straightforward and pretty fucked up. We think there is nothing in it for us. 'Nothing' as far as it goes with material matters, but so much more when it involves the restoration of our being and revitalisation of senses.

We become beams of light shining bright, drawing others attention and appeal, that's right. You are a genuinely good person, **BELIEVE IN IT AND BE IT**.

If we sink into the depth of instant gratification we will deeply depend on the dangerous company of finding fake connections with unruly intentions, emanating from the man-made world. If you follow your spirit, however, it is inexhaustible and will always depend on acts of kindness to flourish from.

When you start to strive to share, rather than strive to self-indulge, a magnetic style aura will allure others toward your vibrations.

The magic you are made of is much more valuable than any other thing you desire on earth. It is priceless and precious in every way; make it your mission to find your magic! We must intend to ignite our soul with sharing so that a community feeling can heal the hate. A great example is what I see in Berlin with protests taking place nearly every weekend. We share our love, power and passion during demonstrations so that politicians and others see how serious we are about caring. Take care of yourself, take care of others, take care of the world. Three things that can't be that hard to render.

Taking care of yourself is something that keeps giving as you feel healthy and happy in doing so. Adopting an attitude that allows you to bloom out of bettering yourself while boosting others initiates inward care to caress your kind nature. Start giving and you will get so much more in return because the power of gentleness can overcome every wickedness.

Greed as a game

When we are so wound up in concerning ourselves with conditional forces such as greed, we indisputably get lost in a game that seems to be out of our control. AKA: lost in a world looking for happiness in all the wrong places. Delusional thoughts and expectations are extended into a whole different line of gab. Imagine greed as an interactive game with levels, where each level is a step closer to this idolised idea of happiness. Recognise that happiness is an idea: it does not involve a medal or a certain amount of points to be won at the end. What is the point of a game where the end goal to reach does not promise any purpose or prize because it does not exist?

The point is that it builds up your ego into self-centred sensations side-tracking you away from self-regulation skills that further you away from your true self and centre your yearnings around false fantasies.

Monopoly could be considered as a worthy example of a game for greed, where components centre their targets around winning as much money as possible. For the sake of imagination, I am not going to use monopoly because it is a game with a lot of studies already behind it to show how levels of wealth increase entitlement of self-interest, so let's just imagine greed as a game: GREEME. It's like a meme ;)

Firstly, using a game as a visualisation of our greed shows that we all participate in a life that does not have any guarantees attached to it. No matter how many plans, purposes or promotions you have in life, something is bound to happen out of the blue because life cannot be structurally planned like building a house or readying a wedding. Greed is omnipresent.

Now more than ever, we are always wanting way more than what is served on our plate, going for seconds, thirds, stuffing ourselves silly. If you play a game of greed, then your ego is only going to become more deafening to what is true and take you further away from the magic you are made of. By nature, our mind is a naturally shining star; if you treat it right then it will shine bright, but if you dilute it with sources of stimulants such as greed then it will suffer as a consequence. You are not your negative thoughts, although sometimes you may believe so.

Back to the game. Each level blinds you a bit more to the truth because immersing yourself into the greed plays a game inside our heads. Each level binds you a bit more to the destructive lies that greed forfeits us to think is the truth. Imagine you are on the level of greed with love: not a materialistic item, but one can become greedy in ways in which we receive love. Jealousy, zealousness and fear forfeit the real love that we are experiencing because all we are concentrating on is getting more love than we think we are being shown.

Secondly, the game is never-ending if there is no final purpose. We might be in control of some things, but when greed is concerned, control is out of the question because it beats up all manners of self-restriction and replaces it with self-indulgence. Greed specifically amuses reassurance and the feeling of safety, because as humans we primarily seek out to feel secure in a mixed-up world. We all work to have money and feel stable. We all want a spouse to share a connection and feel safe. We all want a family to set up a solid foundation of love and not be alone.

We all want to love because it shields us from sadness and seclusion. Simply put: we crave security. That is why greed can grab us and never let us go if we lose track of who we are. We all ache for things in one way or another because it is in our human nature, yet what we must remember is that we are in control of how much we thirst for these things and why. Question your priorities and relieve your anxieties.

When entering into the spiel and all its sections, you get deeper as you get obsessed with excessive amounts of selfishness, climbing up the ladder of egoism. Your main concern is to get more but not be more. The game of greed does not have an end but it does determine an end to your existence, drenching you with a sadness that seems to never be gone. C.S.Lewis said that if a game is played, then losing is possible. Exactly this. When it comes to greed, losing is possible and winning is impossible because you always end up grappling with the constant need to win more and therefore never feel content.

It turns you into a stubborn spirit with an unrepentant heart that beams to boast winds up to be wicked and does not find peace. All your energy is put into looking for something outwardly and not focussing within. The game of greed is like a catch 22 effect, a ceaseless cycle consisting of eternal disappointment and short-lived highs driven by a devotion to own more than you already attain.

Greed misdirects our search for happiness

In the Bible, there are many wise words when it comes to conducting yourself in a humble and honourable fashion. A passage that sticks out to me when considering if greed is heightened by our wicked ways in the world is: "This only have I found: God made mankind upright, but men have gone in search of many schemes." (Ecclesiastes 7:29)

This verse summarises that sin prevails in our search for satisfaction in a whirlwind of wicked ways. Our mentality that is based around societal demands and pressures cheats us to find happiness in all the wrong places. Our effort expended in constantly needing new sources of stimulants is a prime example of just how tormented and tricky our world wants us to covet all the wrong things.

We search in all the shady places because we are shackled to sinful desires that do not dignify our true desires. What if greed were something that we can learn to steer away from? It is. Our continual sense of wanting to control can be modified by replacing fear, anxiety and craving with a right to shine bright through excelling in kindness, gratitude and giving. If God made us upright, then we can source out that spirit by asking him for guidance to restore our real right to be a good and proper person. Whatever your belief or faith is in, let it guide you towards the light.

2 Timothy 3:16 also speaks a truth that "All scripture is god-breathed and is useful in teaching, rebuking, correcting and training in righteousness so that the man of God may be thoroughly equipped for every good work." No matter what you believe in, there has to be something. A guide in being a good person is great, especially during these questioning times we are living.

Whatever your scriptures, quotes or mantras may be, it is great to seek them out because as humans we thrive when we work towards something or follow something because it means you are setting yourself good intentions as well as striving to be someone that is equipped for the sins of the world, such as greed.

You cannot expect a change unless you are going to make one - guide yourself to giving and simmer down on the fascination of the future. Don't crave control, rather succumb to the present.

Greed causes anxiety

Buddha teaches that "Craving brings pain; craving brings fear. If you do not yield to craving, you will be free from pain and fear". Craving is a synonym for greed, and we can learn a lot from what Buddha is bringing forth here. In its basic format- fearful craving causes a great source of pain.

When we are longing for something or someone, we are absolutely absorbed by that feeling, rather overwhelmed by it. This takes us away from being free because we are willingly attaching ourselves to emotions such as pain, fear and anxiety. As stated earlier, it also shows how it is all in the power of our mind. We have the power to overcome greed by getting back in touch with our prosperous propensity to predetermine the way we feel. Like the precepts of the bible, Buddha still bears great significance over our time and ways, if not now more than ever.

Actively seeking out worldly affairs makes your mind overwhelmed with countless choices and decisions, resulting in stress-induced feelings. Our response to wanting more causes worry, especially when we don't receive instant gratification and enter into a pile of panic-driven dealings. Instant gratification gains full force, demanding standards to be entertained, where expectations expand and patience is a thing of the past. We have become so distant to our inner feelings that we rely on this reassurance of greed being beneficial to feeling safe and sound in society.

However, almost always with avid aspirations, we are bound to the feeling of fear because the delusion of thinking of what we need in life limits us. To steer away from stress, pinpoint what it is that is making you stressed, what exactly is the root of the cause and all the stems of stress that stems from that.

The same goes for greed. If you are aware that longing for something is sinking you into a deep pot of misery, then get rid of the catalyst. Sounds easy? It is easy! All it takes is to realise what exactly you want to free yourself from so that you can be free.

Start small think big

As any pattern of behaviour or competing motivations fluctuate and send us into a fluster, greed abides by the same kind of thing. In multiple studies in the science of greed, it is evident to see that the wealthier individual moralises greed as being good. Why so? Simple really when you think about it.

Those who earn more tend to be exclusively focused on their deservingness, sending them into a state of being consumed by what they consume, whereas those who earn less are not consumed by what they earn, rather they besiege and exhibit more empathy for others.

Thus, studies show that the richer the person, the less inclined they are to show a leaning towards donating money to the poor because of the fact they purely pursue their vision of success to the impairment of those around them.

All in all, the quote that the rich get richer and the poor get poorer makes complete sense when we see it from this viewpoint because the wealthier bestow their best interest solely in themselves, dismissing the rest. This then encourages a cascade of negative effects to perpetuate their ego and self-centred ways which will make people less attracted and concerned for that individual.

When one of the world's wealthiest people, Bill Gates, implies that "Humanity's greatest advances are not in its discoveries – but in how those discoveries are applied to reduce inequity" do we realise that injustice is our greatest challenge as human beings. To bring the state of being equal, we must strive to be less greedy and more concerned for humankind. Ultimately, we all crave purpose in what we do. It's because we are here to share and care, not to neglect and disrespect. Anybody can change, no matter if rich or poor, you just have to begin little by little. Start small, think big. Here are five ways in which you can start to bring small but significant changes through psychological interventions:

1) Small changes to values:

Restore empathy and re-think about your values in people and yourself. If you value yourself to be enough then your belief to bring about the best in others will instantaneously spark because of the empathy being exalted through your view of valuing others. Such a simple act of ethics will help you prosper and feel better about yourself in the long run and not be tied down by narcissistic needs. We must attempt to see everyone as an equal without passing judgment. Look but don't judge. Exerting oneself to not be confined to the narrowness of reality incorporated by delusional acts spurred on by society will guarantee a glee and glow to flow from your face, actions and thoughts.

NOW WRITE DOWN 5 WORDS THAT YOU FIND ARE MOST VALUABLE TO YOU.

Mine are curiosity, connection, compassion, gratitude, and honesty.

2) Small gestures can make a big change:

Begin to share rather than hold back. When actively participating in compassionate acts of goodness from your heart, one's faith in humanity is restored. A bigger sense of life is brought to focus when one realises that we are all here for the same reason, sharing the same space, breathing the same air… the list goes on! Restoring faith means hope, love and luck will ensue which are key to planting peace in everyone again. Aim to do 3 small gestures a day for 3 weeks and notice how bright you begin to be.

Shine like the star that you are :)

3) Small ways to contribute to the community:

When one proceeds to do things out of a free will and for nothing in return, then an ecstatic feeling of doing something good will evolve your emotions and enlighten your path to a brighter and happier life. A sense of achievement comes from kindness because you are contributing to the greater good of people and putting other people first. For example, volunteering towards your community in certain ways will generate generosity and spread the spirit of giving as well as bringing advantages in the community. You are here to feel worthy, so use it to your advantage.

4) Small messages mean a lot:

Ever received a one, two or three-word message that has made a massive impact on your day? It has the instant ability to brighten up your day and jolly you on your way, right? A compliment can go a long way. Aim to see the best in people or start easy and see something good in every person who you cross paths with and don't be afraid to tell them what you appreciate about them. Appreciation comes naturally to all of us- use it to make others feel good as well as yourself. Elevating others elates you.

5) Small moments mean more than anything:

Live for the moment and make every minute worth living. Take one day at a time. At the end of the day, it is the fleeting moments and specific seconds that we remember with a certain someone or special people that mean the most. Allow yourself to truly realise that life is all about living in the present moment and making the most out of them with the mindset that all we have is now. It is exactly those moments that will shed light on what is significant in making life worthwhile.

Small nudges in certain directions that activate egalitarianism will remind yourself of what matters and discard the discouraging characteristics and arbitrary acts away. Replace wickedness, stubbornness, and ruthlessness with "glory, honour and peace for everyone who does good." (Romans 2:8). Stop searching outside and start seeking within to restore your hope in humanity and revive your faith in planting peace within.

Small gestures go a long way,

Small compliments make someone's day,

Small moments mean more than anything,

Small connections blossom into the truest thing we know to be real,

Small sentiments season you on your way,

A jolly way to a joyful life staying true with every stride,

Stride to strive,

Strive to thrive,

Thrive to be the beautiful being that you are because life will take you far.

Lastly - exchange greed for glee!

Be happy with what you have. Yes, I know this is easier said than done considering the world we live in impels us to always bend over backwards to want more. Try to be more. Be more by doing more for you. Be more by following your heart. Be more of you in your crazy hazy days or low life ways... emotions are like waves, coming and going. Be more by accepting each wave of emotion and enter into acceptance. All in all, it is achievable by taking tiny steps. Learn to treat yourself like a child, with consideration, care and caution... here is a list that may help you onward and upward:

1. Don't conform to consumerism or it will consume your character.

2. Friends and family lead to fulfilment, not materialistic items: aim to spend more time with people that care about you.

3. You can have it all when you accept, compromise

and move on. Learn to accustom and adjust to things out of your control.

4. Always busying here, there and everywhere? Learn to sit still and just be with your senses more often.

5. Combat greed by caring for those in need.

Little Things

What are the little things?

Little things make you appreciate life that little bit extra. They can be as simple as adoring the smell of rain to admiring someone's style in the street. Petrichor or panoply assigns your attention to focus in on the now and forget about the rest. Noticing little things is effortless.

It is a grand form of gratitude. Appreciation of the finest, happiness at the humblest and amusement in its easiest form. We seem to overlook the little things these days because we are so envious of others' lives, shackled by what people think and self-absorbed by our image in their eyes. Social media has a massive part to play in the making of the "selfie generation". It is like we are clowns that cannot cure our happiness because we essentially seek to amuse others, in the meantime unconsciously ignoring our needs and overlooking the little things for what they are.

Why bypass what the world has to offer? Do not dismiss the delight that simple moments behold in brightening your day or bringing you a source of hope on the way. Little things are all around us. We have just forgotten to look up, look around. Stuck to screens that drain our souls and dismiss our needs. Look up. Stare inquisitively. Smile intentionally. Stride intently. Study the sky, adore its beautiful bluey pink sunset colours or the clouds formations, gathering to shower our streets with water.

Notice how quickly the clouds are passing by as if in a rush to push the plane along or the bird's tweet to each other in the trees, noticing such simple everyday little things concede us to see that we are a part of a bigger picture, bringing you back to peace within. You are the sky. Every other freckle is the forecast. Every breath is a breeze. Every blink is a shooting star. Embody yourself with what is around you and feel alive: that is what brings you back to life. Extract and distract yourself.

If not, it is easy to feel lost, lonely and low. Let the little things find their way through to cheer you up especially when least expected, and share the love by laughter or a kind look; straightforward techniques to find happiness in everyday life. The little things are free and can be anyone's cup of tea. Find your fashion or flair to stare and see things for what they are... and smile!

What are the greater things in life?

Generally speaking, we have categorised the greater things in life as materialistic items and money. Of course, these are not greater things because they are not for free. The best things in life are for free, ever heard that? Well, it's true. Yet, we have become accustomed to consumerist habits that have taken control over us and managed to cloud the true essence of life itself. We have been put on this earth to exist, but to simply exist would be a pity. That is exactly what occurs when we are absorbed by the bigger and supposedly better things in life that taint what is important in life and take us further away from what counts: the small things. Don't let them go unnoticed.

This has been preached to us for decades upon decades, alike the fact that cigarettes are bad for us. Still, similar to smoking warnings, some of us choose to ignore it. We are fully aware of the consequences and what it can lead to, yet we carry on overlooking the reality of how rare and right such simple moments can mean. Sitting on a bench at the park, feeling the sun kiss your cheek or the wind give you a shudder, laughing with loved ones, holding hands with the one... We have all felt it - that natural high.

In effect, ignorance is a form of neglecting your real state of happiness. Society spurs us on to ignore smaller things in life because everything is about wanting more. We are carved and crafted to work until our wit's end whilst neglecting our contentment to heal our heavy-duty emotions and trying thoughts. We are gripped with distress and teased with pain due to daily disorders of the erratic world we live in, leading to suffering.

The root cause of inner suffering stems from us ignoring our peace within, so let us acknowledge ways in which we can turn ignorance into awareness by seeing how the small things that you thought were nothing can mean something, and, may even mean everything. Be aware. Be alert. Enter into the realms of love and light by noticing what is bright and feels right. Begin to actively participate in the life we have been blessed with, by finding joy in the little things that surround us.

If you pursue to pay attention to the small things, you will be able to train your mind to unearth enjoyment in daily life, whenever a fleeting moment or fluttering butterfly passes you.

It naturally heightens your spirits. When we become fully fascinated by finding happiness in a lovely house or a swanky car, the little things are pushed aside and in the end, you wonder what is missing. The true state of felicity is at fault. By cherishing the little things, one will feel uplifted as well as motivated to maintain a life that exhibits excitement and displays delight. Reign in ruling your own life by understanding how precious the priceless and passing moments can be when conveyed with a heart full of grace and gladness. It is these serendipitous situations that act as a basis for being a better person.

The basic foundation of little things is based on bringing awareness to light and converting your sense of happiness into appreciation... for every single thing that seems to show up. See the good in things and you will grow wings.

Smile and laugh: it is that easy

When smiling is involved, an eruption of laughter is bound to evolve. It only takes a matter of time. Smiling can send away the distressed daze, while laughing can cure sadness within an instant. A good laugh is the best cure for anything. It reduces tension in your body and breaks down mental blocks, be it anxiety or depression. A sweet smile is the best remedy to a broken heart. The blessed thing about being cheery is how easy it can be - learn to smile at people, make it a habit.

Anybody can bear a beam upon their face, it is as easy as showering; necessary, but not compulsory daily because it is a matter of choice. Most of the time when walking down the road, I either see people glued to their screen or just looking miserable, so I started to aim my simpler style smile at more people. I am naturally a smiley person anyway, but it showed me two things:

1) Some people are just grumpy and grinning is a rarity for them, so don't take it personally. They will look at you weirdly because it is a rarity for someone to smile for no reason, but it will make their heart warm. You can either be miserable or merry, it is your choice.

2) Smiling at someone may just ignite their mouth to round up into a curve until they seem to be smiling back at you, of which is a great feeling incurred from your free will. It is like you are spreading the magic of being alive. You can be alive but smiling makes you feel alive.

Morgan Freeman said: "There is nothing we can do that can't be done with love."

So, let us spread the love through a smile. Simple. Grinning as you go on with your daily routine is easier than you expect, trust me. After you realise you are sharing a source of elation, you recognise that smiling also automatically makes you feel better. Source out a smile and a chuckle when you notice little things in the streets. This does not imply that you must laugh at people, but be curious and caring when pondering at those going about their day and permit yourself to marvel.

It could be that you see a group of friends having fun in their world with no idea about the goings-on around them (what a great feeling) or somebody helping an elderly person cross the road (what a sweet thing), or even a mother and child giggling at a private joke (ok, the mum could also be shouting at the kid, still smile - could give her the strength!). As you catch a glance of people sharing fits of laughter, helping each other out or happy in each other's company, it is hard not to feel some sort of hope and happiness resonate within you.

That is love. Has your attention ever been caught randomly by a crazy laugh? I love it. I admire it. After all, laughing is infectious. It can catch you out of the blew when you least expect it and all of a sudden, you slip into a burst of merriment that might last for minutes or seconds, but either way, it will make you forget about the fads of the world. When laughter hits, every other emotion valid before is prohibited to partake.

Everything will vanish and be replaced with pure bliss, as you become fully immersed into a bubble of beatitude naturally consenting to whatever wild and wonderful hint of humour it was that gained your full attention. This is the delight in discovering that laughter is the key to letting go. Through the joy of laughter comes the joy in little things. Remember, the tiniest hint of humour can bring spells of serenity, who knows whose day you might make.

It is noted that the average kid laughs 300 times a

day, whereas an adult laughs only five times a day. What an utterly sad statistic, right?! Working with children truly opens my eyes and heart to how humble and happy little people are in their unaffected condition of the world around them. A child takes everything at ease, without a worry in the world, granting their goodness to seep through. A kind act is done without any expectation of it being returned because they genuinely care. A burst of laughter arises out of thin air because their life is a playful stream of creativity and learning. The fact that laughter and love come naturally to children shows us that we are all born with the gift to care unconditionally.

We can learn a lot from the childlike state of mind in terms of not taking everything so seriously... I mean why do you have to take life so seriously anyway? Stop taking yourself so seriously and start to find yourself funny. Sounds silly, I know. It works a treat though! If I do something stupid, then I aim to laugh and the same goes in public.

Laugh it off - make it your mantra and see the positive effect! We are all here to live, but are we all living? Laughing succeeds in making life richer and fuller. Source out laughter and sync in with rapture. Laughing fits with friends, fixing everything and smiles can rise with revelling. Laughter is the natural medicine to happiness, harnessing your sternness in exchange for wittiness. You have the choice to chuckle, cheer up and chase away the dismay.

Accept where you are right now

It truly is the little things that count in life, but most of the time we are too occupied to realise it. We live for the future and forget about now. Those seconds you shared with someone stick with you, absorbed by them in every way. Those minutes that made you laugh, make your heart warm when looking back. Those hours spent with loved ones, fully present in their company with no thought of what is to come. All of these flashes of time have something in common that count towards an incomparable emotion, never to leave you when reminiscing: the reminder of how it made you feel.

You may forget a conversation or a location, but you will never forget the way a person made you feel. Smile and laugh back about it to yourself. It is easy enough to forget what people said or did, but you will never fail to remember their impact, printed on your heart for a purpose. Impressions last a lifetime. Feelings stay with us because they essentially make us, especially the truly taunting and treacherous downers, but also the elated and ecstatic euphorias. Dependent on what kind of person you are, if you either dwell on the past and bad times, or if you prefer to treasure moments of joy that have touched you with gladness, the effect of reminiscing could be hurtful or honourable.

Profit from recollecting memories by being cheerful and grateful for having lived and learnt. Don't be sad that it is over, be glad that it took place and now you are in another place, learning to embrace. The main problem with looking back persists in staying in the past. One must not dwell on memories in a nostalgic yearning to relive them or wish to go back to them, yet understand that these moments were beautiful in that exact time and space. Be proud that you survived them.

Be pleased that you experienced them. Be positive that you are the person you are right now because of the past. Memories mould us into the people we are right now. Be it bad or good, we are all easily taken away with recollections of the past at some point. It can be hard to be happy, it can be hard to know how you even feel about them. Just let it be. Memories are there to remind us of how strong we are. Memories are there for us to reflect, revive and redefine.

Memories can make you feel a rollercoaster of emotions, that is the way it is. Try to remember that each feeling is fleeting so it is OK to recall, but don't feel like you have hit a wall. Look back and smile. Laugh. Cry. Prompt the feeling that you experienced at that moment and confess to its vibrations, how extraordinary life can be. The key is to not get attached to something that has already been lived. Remove the emotional bond compelling you to yearn for "better days" by accepting where you are right now. Be patient. Be hopeful. That was then and this is now, so accept and move on. Little moments live forever, grasp and engage with this fact so you can glance back, but look forward.

Wherever and whatever you are living right now is what matters the most. There is nowhere that you shouldn't be. Anywhere could be where you are meant to be, so don't think that you "ought " to be somewhere else because you will forget about the now.

Now is all we have. Take in you and your surroundings, see how you can make now mean the most and make the best of what you have. Your home is where your heart is. Your home is not physical, it is a feeling. You can make a home wherever you like. Home is not always a place, a home can also be a face. Home is looking inward and forgetting about outward. Do not try and race, a home cannot be chased. It can be found in a person or a place or just looking in the mirror at your face. Look inward and find a home in your heart by consulting your inner wisdom.

Unfortunately, we have built buildings over our natural environments, making it difficult to determine true happiness in such urbanised structures. We get bored with building blocks, scared by skyscrapers and tormented by traffic, which in turn affects our well-being for the worst. Life can be testing. One of the main attributes to happiness in adults is how beautiful they find the city they live in. This shows how we all have an inherent need for beauty because it makes us jubilant. You should feel happy with your neighbourhood and where you live, if not, you might not be serving your happiness to its full potential.

Sometimes it isn't simple, so solicit surroundings near you that you find pretty, find peace. You should be able to feel at ease or at least find serenity in your place of peace. You can make *anywhere* your home, you just have to make it your comfort zone. Environments that are aesthetically pleasing place a strong impact on our well-being, heightening our spirits and providing a sense of belonging. Decorate your house, buy some candles, put photos up, get a house plant, make anywhere you live your home by partaking in making a room yours with pretty paraphernalia.

We all have this longing to feel at home, yet what we don't realise is that the milieu has a massive influence in this longing. The same goes for people: if you surround yourself with people you like, then you will be happy. If you surround yourself with pretty places, parks, open spaces etc. then you will be happy.

It is all down to you, nobody chooses for you. You choose where your home is, so let it be a place full of warmth and joy, on the inside and out. If you live near a park, or a field, make the most of it. Take your time to go out and stroll singly, smile at little things that you come across en route. Even if you live in a big city miles away from mountains or fields, it is vital to take that time out to travel to such serene places and ponder on how it makes you feel to be truly alive.

Nature has always got your back. When we get bored, we must move and make the most of free time to liberate ourselves from the structure set out by society and social media, so that we can tune in with ourselves and disengage with senseless scrolling. If you learn to love where you are, when you are, then a special connection occurs, that of peace and acceptance for the now. Embrace if you cannot escape. Through accepting and appreciating your daily views, you undoubtedly will find joy in the little things.

Stumble across serendipity. We all have an inherent need for beauty. Embrace it. Live it. Consider nature to be your friend in need- always there and ready to revive you in times of need. OK, so some of us are not fortunate enough to live close to a national park or a forest, but we all have a hint of nature to run away to. Utilise what you have on offer to the best of your ability and aim to feel united with wherever you are at. Accept it and live it.

Train your brain to notice what's around yourself

Listen and look poem:

Pay attention to what is around you, like the sky when it is so blue.
Don't hesitate to take heed in what you need, it doesn't take much to be freed.
Who cares for what you crave, make the best with what you save.
Count your blessings daily, it's for your sanity mainly.

Concentrate on what you have and not what you don't have,
think of it like this: the less you wish, the more you cherish.
Be grateful for your simple fairy tales and fall in love with the details.

Listen and look.

It's like crossing the road but incorporated into everyday life. Awareness. Concentration. Mindfulness. Whatever you want to call it, bringing a sense of alertness into daily routines inspires gratitude, honour and enjoyment to transpire. Being alert makes life lush and sparks your spirit of eagerness. All it involves is awareness - it is about using your sight, smell and touch to be active in the life you're living. Just as you are taught as a child to stop, look and listen when crossing the street, the same rule applies in the daily comings and goings. Just like a dog or a cat, be carefree because there is no fee, it is the easiest way to spark curiosity. Your eyes are open every day, so be thankful for the gift of sight.

You taste without trying, you hear without miming. Optimise the way you perceive things and the world will reveal its charm. Adopting this open approach will take away the strife of the mundane get-up-and-go show and replace it with stillness, connection and trust. Just look and listen. Directly participate in your life and become conscious of how it is shaping your attitude and presence.

When you listen and look at all that is around you, stillness can be found in your essence. When you listen and look at everything, there is a force that connects you and your spirit with your surroundings, instilling worthiness and meaning into your soul. When you listen and look, the power of love shows you there is more to life than to cooperate as a robot in the rat race of routinist chores.

Surrender to fear and embrace the fun. Life is fun if you make it, only depends on the way you see things. The first step in awakening to what is around you: Open your eyes.

Look up! We tend to ignore and miss out on the hidden beauty in things that circulate us. In the midst of it all, we lose out on a sensation evoked through the way a lane is lit up or the puddle's reflections on a rainy day.

There is so much in the street to see! Street art, birds, cathedrals, skyscrapers, street names… the list goes on and when attracted to such centrepieces will you realise all the missing pieces open up your heart and mind to a different dimension of appreciation.

Your perspective will open up, heightening alertness and awareness when noticing things, encouraging you to keep on going and restoring faith in life. Street art is a special favourite of mine and I love how it exists everywhere I go, peaking out in all its diverse shapes and forms with hidden messages and activist intentions. When you spot a piece of street art – stop and look.

Stop and appreciate the art, but mainly stop and ponder on the message. What does the artist want you to see? What does it mean for you? When you actively partake in taking the time to look at things on the street, especially art, it makes you wonder and drift into higher consciousness.

Art is to be appreciated. Art is life. It is all around us, it is only up to us to notice it, learn from it. The special thing about street art is that it will stick with you. Some street art may take a great effect on your impression and perception of a topic, or it may open your mind up to another world not been considered before, or even enlighten you on the heated topic of our world, as we go on our way and unconsciously contribute to its suffering.

It can spark a cultural awareness and allocate an understanding within, where you are in a deeper and more sentimental sense of being connected to the place, be it a city, town or village. It is all about lighting up an awareness that you can grow from within. Look and learn. Build on what you see on the street to show you more meaning in life and adore all its variety and venture.

The little things could be waiting for you to notice them right on your doorstep, you're just not looking properly because it gets to the point where our environment becomes normalised. We take it for granted. Inhabiting a long-term residence may take the exoticism out of the little things. That is normal. Switch it up. Start looking at things like it is the last time you will see them in your life and an appreciation will freely form, incomparable to that of everyday living.

Imagine it is your last day on holiday, trying to soak in every last bit as much as possible. Alternatively, see things as if for the first time, taken away by the sheer charm, humbled to be a part of the experience. Marvel at the way you feel blessed to be present in a certain place. Be content, admire looking and feeling the ambience as it amplifies your aura to want to share what you see with others.

Share the love. Take your leisure in looking at things, begin to adore the way it makes you feel like you belong. Be content to take a stroll at one's leisure looking through every hidden corner and closed door. You are at a state of ease and comfort, a feeling we closely relate to as "home". All these sauntered countries and cobbles become a part of you and become pieces of your heart. Home is a feeling.

Seeing the change in yourself when returning to familiar spots shows how places don't change, only the people. Feel worthy when wandering through streets that you are familiar with, as it ignites a sense of security. Replace emptiness with worthiness. Let locations light up the love stored within. Feel honoured to harbour your eyesight. Flourish from it, meaning lies in everything. Your life compares to a show, this episode is saved as an experience you'll look back on and smile. Smile because it happened. Smile because you are taking time to truly live with what you call home.

One of the most uncomplicated forms of feeling fully cognizant of life is to be grateful for what you have got, so open your eyes up in a new and fresh way every day. Learn to look. Look to learn.

Use whatever you see as a way to marvel in your magical manner. Imagine life as a museum, a 24/7 exhibition for your eyes only. Imagine life through a baby's eyes: uncensored, untamed, open to the world. Imagine life through a dog's eyes: cool, calm and playful. Scan around with an inquisitive eye.

Stimulate yourself in self-realisation. Make it a daily "chore" to discover something new in the street or recognise random happenings unravelling around you, be it a squirrel scurrying up the tree or the sun peeking through, and your spirit will gradually grow by what you view.

After a while, looking up, down and all around will become a part of you and you will perform it candidly. Engage in your sight and be filled with might. You are entering inwardly, the essence of you beams through as you act mindfully, being present in your presence with nature. You are unleashing your inner identity as you notice the things around you are all connected. We are all connected on a level so much deeper than we think, use it to restore your strength.

When you see the world with awe and an active state of mind, it is easier for the mental noise to be hushed because it is dismissed through forcing concentration elsewhere, in this case, to what is on the outside. It also enables you to locate love on the inside because it is present practice. Tune in with yourself on the inside as a means to capsize the ability of an overworking mind to manipulate you. We are all slaves to overthinking, so remedy it with drifting, going with the flow. Look higher and light up within. Freely enter into the gateway of gratitude because everyone sees something distinct in their own eyes.

This opens the door to being more. Being is better than having. Every day is different – enjoy the discovery of sight during day and night. Everything is readily available for interpretation, it is just up to you to wake up and open your eyes. The glance of a baby beholds a new universe, the way it looks at you with purity, curiosity and entitles you to feel spiritual prosperity.

Listen out! You could hear that laugh as mentioned before, or kids playing, ducks quacking, people singing: step back from your headspace sound, noise pollution and just listen to what is beckoning at you to be heard. It can be natural elements as much as human elements; the mixture makes life better. Listening out to peals of laughter or high pitched voices brings back hope in humanity. Restore it through being there, being aware.

Hear the river gush at the side and all the trees wave in the breeze, feel the weight release. Stress subsides as nature brings back hope. All in all, listening out distracts the mind from listening in to the whispers, relocating your stability and strength. It is true to say that noise pollution is something we do not intentionally listen out for, but it does perplex the senses nonetheless, causing stress and imbalance in mind and body.

Noise pollution consists of cars, construction work, lorries and the lot. It is a health issue that we are ignoring, especially for those who live in big cities. It sends shivers of shocks to the system as it covets stillness during sleep, overall damaging our will to work as a functional and fit human being. Traffic torments the senses, whereas trees tantalize them. Escape to the forest or nature reserves as and when you can, so that you may find peace in placing yourself first. It has been found immersing yourself in trees can cause anti-cancer cell activity to occur. If the forest is far away, then the blissful things about cities are that parks are always available to sit and stay still in. Find your serenity.

Music matters

   Stick your music in and let the vibrations take you on a ride. Music is magical, it can distract or direct you dependent on what, why and when you tune in. Listen and let go. Sound in, world out. Hear the music, feel the pain or turn off your inner rain. Music is a marvellous way to reflect, retain or raise spirits. It can be so soothing to the ears when you require it or rhythmic when you are ready for it. Listening to a specific song can cause an array of emotions to take over, sending your body and mind into a state of sanity. Music is a gift, it can rewire your "what is life" and answer your whys?

   I find it quite astonishing how a song can take you back to a certain place or trigger a feeling, one already completely forgotten about. Music is magic. Use it to ignite your virtue within to fade out the noises without when it gets too much. Plugging in your earphones is easy peasy. Deliberately tune into a song, swallowing up your devout attention to nothing but the present moment. Let the rhythm ride your interest; walk with purpose, accredit the beat to bring a head nod, the lyrics accentuate your awareness in being alive, and the combination of sounds secure a smile on your face. Sing out loud, feel proud.

Get involved with the magnetism music offers, like laughter it is at our service for free. Completely absorb yourself in songs or have it as a background engagement. When the volume is low, the mind is still distracted by distant noises that prod for your recognition, yet you possess more control over what is your focal point. A baby crying. A car beeping. Look around and see that life is happening around you, no matter what. Use your ears to amplify the acknowledgement of your atmosphere and feel no fear.

Go dancing, let loose. Go to a concert, let go. Go to a musical, listen in. Either way, attending musical events confess a connection within and without you to occur, bringing meaning, soul and life to the vision. You feel connected, worth appears as you relate to lyrics or relax with mixes. You are united with harmonies and symphonies as you are banded together with beats and booms. You are music. Permit melodies to make you feel whole again, rhythms to ride your heavy tide of stress into the distance, mixes to manage your emotions - up, down and all around just like your waves of woes.

Music is life, use it to get rid of strife. Have that one song you require to regain strength or another song that raves with you being down. Employ music to ride the rhythms of your emotions, engage with music to bring meaning back, enable music to show you your worth.

Ever so stressed that you could shout and scream?
Breathe in and out, shake it all about,
maybe do the hokey pokey or whistle a lil remedy,
hum a tune, make yaself swoon,
sing a song, ring a gong, wriggle away what feels wrong
simply remember your favourite melody,
make it feel like your own remedy,
whistle, sing or hum away from the blues aboard the healing cruise.

Interact and distract

Interacting with others encourages you to regain self-worth, be it with an animal or a human being. We all know that socialising with people provides a present moment feeling that cannot be disturbed (unless phones are on loud!). We are currently cohabiting a technology-driven crisis that causes socialising to sometimes be more strenuous for us to dedicate our full-blown time to. Why? Phones intrude. Before meeting people, have an Instagram session or scroll through Facebook relentlessly and let it all out. When you're with people, intend to be in their full presence, it is only cooperation. With some people, you don't have to even contemplate taking your phone out, but with others you do. It's OK. Everyone deserves the time of day, as do you. Value others as you want to be treated.

One can simply enjoy the little things when walking a dog, for example. Your dog is your companion, so let yourself learn from it. When walking a dog, recognise its excitement at the sight of another canine or how its tail wags when barking, ready for the run! Utilise the privilege of owning a pet to your best ability – let them show you what the little things can be. Imagine you are living life through your pet's eyes and mind; all it is genuinely bothered about is eating and sleeping. Eat, sleep, repeat.

Dog or rabbit, pets are purely preoccupied with its substance and that is pretty much it. Even at that "worry", it does not seem to bother them whether the food will show up or not, whether tomorrow you will walk it or not, it just lives in the moment. Be happy over food.

Be thankful for food, just as a dog eagerly yaps over it. Be glad for the food on your plate, like a cat purrs and pleasures itself in licking every last bit up. Be grateful for the food you have got, just as a fish fights for the scatterings over the water. Change your mindset about food – like a lot of things, we take it for granted, especially in the fast-food frenzy that has hit everywhere. Eat with intention. Interact with your food and find that recognition prompts thankfulness. If not, little things blur into the distance.

We are constantly distracted through numerous ways, mostly technology-driven devices. Such distractions have commanded our attention towards people, work, and even ourselves into screens. It is considered normal if someone checks their phone right in front of you. We are bored so much easier these days due to the endless amount of distractions that deter us away from being here, right now, reading.

Even when I read (and I love it and set a time to do it every day) there will be some point when I have the urge to make a cup of tea or check my phone.

We have normalised the fact that we cannot concentrate for long, but we are to blame because technology taints our ability to be fully aware. Our modern society is spurred on by purchasing this, that and the other. Anything is possible, as far as the market makes us believe. Our home screens have so many shows that we end up scrolling through what to watch in the amount of time something takes to watch.

Why? We are not satisfied. We are bored. Eventually, when finding a program to put on, one can sit there brainwashed for hours, no need to think, no need to communicate. Where next? We are curving communication to find it online with people we don't even know...

Pay attention to the people that matter the most

Don't forget about those who are your nearest and dearest. Take a minute to message them when you crave that cig or call someone at the end of your day. It is crucial to take care of our

connections.

Cook and brighten up

Distract yourself in healthier and happier ways that influence your creativity to take shape or your relationships to bloom. Distract yourself by cooking and baking! It is a great way of gaining self-awareness. Take pride in making food for pleasure. A plate of food you have cooked is like a product of your love. When consuming the love you have laid out, it is truly a fulfilling experience (in both ways!).

Furthermore, if cooking for other people, then the feeling of being united over something that has come from your heart is one of the littlest biggest things that I, personally, cherish. I love cooking for myself and others because I enjoy the process and waiting. Eagerness and excitement entertain me when waiting.

Then, having the time to tuck in with loved ones is my littlest big thing because it is the time I truly feel connected, humbled and grateful for food, family and friends all at once. An overwhelming feeling of present power fills my heart with love. It is like Christmas day – time to spend with people you love the most and food completes it, come on now, everyone knows it!

It is crucial to interact and distract your dreamy state of mind. Embrace a hearty decision in taking time to interact, distract and delight in the little things. Find out what your little things are by jotting down what you truly enjoy about life at its purest state without any money, job or materialistic items included in the concoction. Be minimalistic. This is about you. Make it your mission to keep the classic things close - focus on making them meaningful and magical in your style. The little things are influential in our happy state of mind. It can be as simple as waking up to see the sunrise, going on a walk or listening to music.

When something small becomes big

Small gestures go a long way because small compliments make someone's day,

Small moments mean more than anything as small connections blossom into the truest thing,

Small sentiments season you on your way because feeling good does not mean you have to pay,

Be on your jolly way to a joyful life, staying true to every stride,

Stride to strive, strive to thrive, thrive in being alive,

Thrive being the beautiful being you are, remind yourself, now and then, here and there, it's only fair.

Fair to be you and fine to come through.

Society as a saturated fat

To stay in the know, you have to be in the show. What show? The show by society - a priority.

You must keep up or you will seem like a lost pup. Technology drives us to be a wuss of what is real and rather leads us to steal.

Fancy shoes, expensive cars, who is even arsed?

Care for free time, coffee time, dinner time, take your time to be with those who are and those who are in spare, spare of a helping hand or a missing strand.

Shine your light and be the light.

Nature

What does it mean to let nature-nurture?

To nurture means to care for, and nature delivers exactly that through a copious amount of formats, such as food and forests. Nature nurtures us every day, without us even realising. Nature is nurturing. Immersing yourself in nature entails an enriching and enlightening effect on your feelings, thoughts and state of consciousness. It is time for the mind, body and soul to reconnect, revive, restore together in harmony. Nature nurtures your mind, body and soul without any extra duties for us to undergo. Sit. Walk. Run. Be still. Look and listen. Nature puts things into perspective. Natural environments reset our minds and bodies through its unique power of relieving stress and heightening mental wellness. Nature is always there for you because nature never says no.

See nature as a friend that you can go to in desperate times of need to notion ease, only possible to ignite through being around God's creation. Nature can be any type of landform, from rivers to beaches or mountains to parks. Many studies have proven that natural environments, such as waterfronts and beaches can reap more benefits to humans than built urban environments and entertainment venues.

Not surprising really, eh? So why are we sitting around on our arses or a treadmill waiting for results to happen to our body when our soul isn't in it? Nature lets you focus on what's true and let go of what's trivial. Connection to nature comes naturally to us all and does not require any. Effort. at. All. Many health and mental issues derive from disconnection to nature.

Distance ends lives whereas closeness cures them. Human beings need nature to restore happiness and revive health, but our society makes us see differently. Civilisation is distancing us from this basic requirement and instead pushes us to the limit, pushes us to sign up to gyms, pushes us towards the pharmacy counters, pushing us further away from the most natural remedy remotely known as nature. Nature has an incomparable ability to heal, so let us discover exactly how and why.

Why nature?

First and foremost, nature is always readily available for us to gain peace and clarity. How? Look at a tree, smell a flower, feel the power. These little things have turned nature into something we take for granted. The natural environment is slowly decreasing because of our urban grey environment taking over. We know that Mother Nature gives us sustenance to live. She sustains us. She nourishes us. Our lives depend on it. Yet we still destroy it bit by bit. Allow nature to take you back to you, so you will know how to get through. Nature has an undeniable strength in bringing you back to your nature, through its craft to settle your mind and access stillness from within. It is this silent and serene state of mind that arouses the genuine serenity in which we find peace.

"We can never have enough of nature" transcendentalist of his time, Henry David Thoreau, pleasantly puts it.

Seeking nature out as comfort is spontaneously stimulating for the mind and body because nature gives back what our man-made environment has taken away: life in its raw form. Life before there was no life. Life as it is. There have been a plethora of studies showing how beneficial it is to besiege oneself with wildlife and natural spaces. As humans, we can adore the formations of the forest with an untamed excitement, a naive child state of delight. No added extras. We are captivated by the radiance of sun rays glimmering on a river. Watch the way water suddenly ripples when a duck dips its beak underneath, a fleeting moment witnessed only by you, one which seems to have occurred solely for your eyes to have glimpsed in that instant. Look at the way the colour of the sky is soothing for your eyes, every sunrise and sunset a sight to behold and marvel at, no matter how many times or where.

Take the time to reflect and realise that you are

going with the flow and letting go. Nature brings beauty in its unadulterated appearance. We do not have to force ourselves to feel something because our undirected attention is accessed. It is effortless. Moments in nature mean the mental effort is not necessary. Your sense of self is seasoned by the landscape, just like a plain meal is enhanced with salt and pepper, bringing a flavour to favour your palate and provide enjoyment. With nature, you notice there is more to life. It forces you to feel full again, as does a meal. Nature does not demand anything from us unlike the daily draining dealings and bleak buildings do, which all the more makes natural territory tantalizing.

   I was blessed to be brought up with the black forest featured as a predominant part in my seasonal visits to my grandparents' home. One of my earliest memories was walking in the forest and a feeling of absolute awe flooding me, of which I could not comprehend. Such tall trees towering over me and a never-ending path tucked within the tall trunks seemed like a dream that I did not want to wake up from, but rather get lost in. As the trees overlooked me, I realised how small I was. It was a great realisation that reality did not matter at this moment in time. This was my reality. Right here. Right now I am in the forest and I am alive. I felt fulfilled with gratitude when admiring the magnitude of trees that taught me I am not alone as I bathed myself in the power of nature. I felt like I was a part of a precious environment that I wanted to take care of and be a part of.

I felt protected by the pines and sheltered by the oaks. If you haven't guessed it by now, yes I am a nature lover, but I never fully realised until I was in my twenties, exactly how much I missed going back regularly as I randomly craved a "Waldspaziergang", a walk in the forest. I am a dendrophile, and you could be also. (Aka a person who loves trees and forests!). It brings me joy that the German language has taken note of how important such an activity is with a word assigned to it especially! I would love going on a Spaziergang with my dear Opa, who would enlighten me about the names of trees and what birds we could hear. It is true when I say that I found myself in the forest when it came to facing my fears or taking on my emotions. It was indistinguishable. Exhilarating. Eye-opening.

Astonishing... that when I went I would yearn to be alone with my feelings and find out how to handle them. Be still. I would wander off on my own from a young age, quickly pottering off ahead of my family (insisting that I was the leader), so that I could fully immerse myself into the magical mood that overtook me whenever I trod foot into the forest. I had this urge to be alone when I entered the forest. It was like a fever that aroused me and called me to fully emerge myself so that I could concentrate on the echoes of the trees ruffling in the wind, or the sounds of the leaves dropping down, rustling and raring to be free from the constraints of its origin.

My time was nature time in the forest. What is your nature time? We all need it, that is for sure. Find out what a forest can do for you when you fully find yourself looking up and reaching out.

Watch the birds fly - you don't have to try,

listen to the rustle of the trees - allow it to make you feel at ease,

sit on the earth below you - let the energy go through you,

gain clarity from the greenery - baffle yourself with its beauty.

Begin to open your eyes to what is real, brighten your spirit and see how you feel.

TREE MEDITATION: Take a second to *gaze at a tree in gratitude and see how you feel *

   If you want to feel free then find yourself in a forest! Get lost outwardly and get in touch within. Everybody suffers at some point with the struggles and strains of society wishing to extract themselves from urban settings and busy streets. Everyone has the opportunity to do exactly this. Distract yourself from the distresses and replenish your exhaustiveness. The Japanese practically prescribe the forest as a therapy in what they call shinrin-yoku, otherwise known as forest bathing. Who knew that prescribing a wander in the woods was established as a therapy in Japan some forty years ago already! "Forest bathing" has been scientifically proven to boost your well-being.

   It is a natural therapy based on the simple concept of strolling through the forest while taking in all the elements for the benefit of your health and happiness. Guess what? It works! The wonders of this work only invite the quality of healing to manifest into your life, as you discover that cultivating connections with nature are the finest that are given to us on this Earth for free.

Engage with your environment

Your surroundings have a massive impact on your mood and magic. It has been proven that we are bound to be a happier person when living in surroundings that we appreciate. The environment we inhabit is not only to be a living space but somewhere for us to communicate, console and connect with, where we should not hesitate to explore.

Through spending time in nature and taking its value in, will we only be able to fully reflect and revive ourselves; life can be enriched to its full capacity as intended. God created nature for us to connect with. So why aren't more of us realising that our medicine is outside and rely on pharmaceuticals rather than fanciful forests? We do not have the time. We do not stop and be still with our surroundings as often as we ought to. It will show you a lot about yourself as you come to identify with nature, letting go of any previous preoccupations your mind could have been revelled in and *focus on the now*. Stop. Stay still. Look around you and let yourself be fully immersed into the moment with nature, acknowledging life in its purest form.

Tree loving

Let us adore the longest living organism on earth – the tree. Concentrate on its existence and identify with it to feel connected. Imagine how much they have seen and sheltered so far in their lifetime, firmly rooted in one place perceiving people over tons of years. Look up to the tree and tell yourself you can be as steadfast and strong. Encounter the tree as a boost of brightness and stimulant of resilience. Stand tall and blow in the breeze but be grounded and grow.

Such a simple method of associating yourself rooted in nature encourages belief to build within and find peace. This form of fixation as well as fixing yourself within the world you live in can be a form of meditation, directing your attention to the tree and its totality. Relating yourself to a tree will enhance the elevation of nature in its nurturing power, without even having to physically do anything. Tree hugging is a thing and can be a source of empowerment. When hugging a tree, the hormone oxytocin is released to flood your body with a state of calmness, serotonin and dopamine are also in the mix excelling in a happier mood. Tree hugging could be considered a natural therapy, so why not try it out using this analysis in mind.

Flower power

Another method might simply be to look at a flower and admire its shades, symmetry and scent. Pay particular attention to its form and colour, muse on its magnitude and charm through its attractiveness. Every flower blossoms and diminishes. We are so similar to flowers if we take their life cycle into account. We like to be admired, we flourish when fed, and we sleep at night to restore our energy. We are all flowers, waiting to grow from what is given and shown to us, yet some of us do not participate in this part of the cycle because we are not shown appreciation, love or compassion from others or even ourselves. If so, we can bloom to be as beautiful as we aspire to be. It is easy to forget about yourself in the midst of it all, as it is with daily watering plants. Apply attention to yourself as you do your plants and learn from it. Learn from the way you treasure your plants and treasure yourself similarly.

   Water yourself with kindness, look at yourself with interest, speak to yourself with caution and compassion. We forget to shower ourselves with self-care and end up diminishing in the dark, just as a plant does. If we take care of our plants, then they will not shrivel up and die. If we learn to show ourselves this love then we also will not wither. Thus, doctors recommend the scenery and surroundings to be a fine form of restoration. It has even been said that gardening enhances longevity and promotes well-being.

   Taking care of what is the source of life and then being able to eat from it provides a connection to nature. Look up and cheer up when observing nature. Acknowledge that the Earth is so immense and you are small, but all the while you matter. Next time you go outside, pleasantly ponder at the plants and trees as we co-exist and continue to employ awareness in everyday life. Let the feeling of being alive bring calmness and consideration for what is around you and what is within you, it all matters.

Most of the time during daily commotions, we are swept off of our feet by being on the go, worrying about the future and filling in the silent moments with overthinking. We turn to our mind-boggling technology, from binge-watching series to wasting time aimlessly scrolling through social media. Instead, take time to separate yourself from the get-go and let go. Disconnect. Take that time out. Set a time to BE your time out... otherwise, it is harder to stick to. Detach yourself, even momentarily. It may make your day as you muse at the sun shining through the window, watch the sun rays glimmer, shimmer and subside offering peace of mind. Listen. Take in the sound of the rain: it can be somewhat soothing to the mind. When you take a moment to meander through the field or wander through the forest, a burst of inspiriting energy will jolly you along your way. Gain from your terrain. Nature can also deliver the same sort of drive a cup of coffee can by buzzing in a present moment awareness of what is around. Simply spending time outside can heighten your spirits, even if it is for ten minutes.

Taking time out in the forest is particularly believed to be beneficial in many marvellous ways, clearly confirming how our bodies effortlessly thrive off being in nature. Walking in the woods is a wondrous way to heal your mind and body, where one can roam freely. Our cells get excited, releasing dopamine and redeeming our conscious cycle of breath. A study shows 54% of cancerous cells are eliminated when being immersed in the forest- how fantastic?!

This is when you realise that nature is always ready to nurture. Not just anyone, but you. Fully grasp that you are not alone within the wilderness, but find your wild side. No matter what, nature is always there for us (pretty amazing when you think about it). Freely wander outside to feel revived, restored and revitalised with the beauty that nature has on offer.

When nature isn't in reach...

It is all well to be notified that nature is there for you, but some of us aren't as delighted by nature as others. Finding joy in little things does not necessarily have to entail trees if we are not so hippy and happy to readily heal ourselves. You may not be physically or emotionally inclined to go out to get your tonic of wilderness and instead, prefer a gin and tonic. Let's see it from a different perspective – beer gardens. What better place to come together with mates and enjoy a drink… or two.

Growing up in the UK made these beer gardens seem like a little hideout or escape for people to let go of their day's dismay to me. Pretty much all local pubs or restaurants have these open patios with the traditional wooden benches and chairs to gather around with surrounding play areas and trees for shelter. Especially in my uni years, I was taken away by how much a cider on a terrace or back yard at someone's place could put me at ease almost instantly (I am not recommending a drinking habit here but setting a scene with buddies to relax!). Whenever the sun peeped out, people would steer themselves towards these outdoor areas like it was your backyard.

   The sun makes a massive difference, everyone knows it, where the simple but sanitising thing of sitting outside with friends can be pure bliss. The social side to it is important, yet the setting holds meaning too. Congregating outside in nature means you are not only connecting but surroundings too. Spain is the same – everyone gathers outside bars with tapas and drinks, relishing in each other's company. It is one of the things that attracted me to live in Spain (sure I'm not the only one!) and embracing this way of life truly fuelled my spirit with positive vibes. This outdoor yearning for cleansing can be found in every city and town, where social spots are attractive to the eye, making you forget "why".

During these scenes of enjoyment, we seem to take it for granted because when something becomes a habit, one sinks into the normalisation of it all. Step out of the circle. Take a look from the outside and see how cool it is to have the chance to leisurely sit outdoors at your "local" sipping away on something and being in the presence of pals, all magically making everything OK, cleansing your palate and giving you a purpose. Letting go can be found in simpler ways than we reckon and this is one of them.

Utilise it to your benefit by taking in the fact that the natural environment enables you to feel a complete calmness when in good company.

Geographical aspects are all around us, so make the most of them! You might be a city person and not a country creature at heart, yet you can find peace on offer anywhere and everywhere you go. How about that drink after work in the beer garden? Go for it. You might need it more than you realise because irritation caused by environmental change is instilled within us all.

    Solastalgia, so it has been named, is now taking over more than ever, instilling trauma and stress within us all, due to the boundless amounts of ugly grey buildings that are not appealing to the eye and make us sigh. So what do we do when the burden of city life gets to us and escaping to nature is not possible?

    There are a myriad of ways in which one can find stillness through all the sounds of a noisy city. Do not be afraid by the hustle and bustle that baffles your instincts to maintain a tranquillity that is sought from within. We can make anywhere we live the best place to live through our intuitive perspective. Look up from your phone. Let your surroundings speak to you. Let us consider a day-to-day situation: the commute to work.

No matter what form of travel, a street will always be involved.

Imagine you are walking down a hectic street with heaps of people going about their own business. Now address the fact that every person is an entity. Create a sense of curiosity, step away from the animosity. Recognise individuals and the way that they are engrossed in their daily lives. Positively ponder at people and let it prod at your perspective of the world. Open your mind to perceive people in a way of authentic appreciation, placing hope in our hearts for the human race. Permit your perspective to broaden for the better, taking on optimism about our environment rather than acclimatising to sinister news content that our society curses us with to heighten hatred rather than encourage acts of kindness.

Be enraptured by someone on a phone call with a loved one, let it lift your spirits by the way that they smirk and blush as love cheerily carries them on throughout their day. Notice the old lady crossing the road that may need assistance and if so, help her out, or see someone else give her a helping hand, spreading the power of compassion, which certainly made her day and will restore your faith in humanity for viewing the act of mercy. Commit random acts of kindness without a second thought, just as it arises from human instinct. Be encouraged by a person lost in their music, absent to the world around them and feel empowered by the mysterious way that music facilitates us to escape into our own world at any time, any place, anywhere. Observe the delighted dog, obediently walking next to its owner, unscathed by the antics around it, so lost in its life, yet so connected to nature. Now adopt the chirpy spring in its step and see how walking with a conscious merriness may make you feel more restful. Appreciate the little children running around without a care in the world and attempt to take on that naïve kind of energy.

Smile. Smiling as a source of appreciation will automatically make you feel some sort of joy, in fact, smiling on its own will grant you gladness to be alive. It is known that if you are to smile at yourself in the mirror every day, you will learn to feel confident in yourself by igniting inner-strength that every one of us has stored within. People just need to smile more! It is so easy and effective. Beaming your grin at somebody else is such a simple act of kindness that can cure bitterness for a split moment and share positive vibes between people bound to spread. I am not saying that smiling can cure all the evil in the world, nor am I advising that a smile will instantly make you feel ecstasy. It is indisputable that you cannot be happy about every little thing you address on the street, but how you see it is what matters most. Help a homeless person out. Give them a sandwich, the one you got free as a deal from the supermarket.

Make someone's day and make yourself see that the little things are the biggest. Your open approach to living is what stimulates your senses to seek out the good in everyday life.

Let us return to meditate on the open perspective impelled by the naivety of a child and excitement of a dog. Simply by being aware of your surroundings, you will adhere to a fresh mentality that may help you see the world differently. Don't ever refrain from people watching; it is a wonderful thing. It opens your mind and puts things into perspective. Ponder.

Sonder. Refrain from trying so much and simply be. Feel your energy. When you stumble across a homeless person, see them for who they are: an average human being like you and anyone else on this earth. We judge too much and don't accept enough.

   Look at them as you do a passing cloud - observe without discrimination. Smile at them and feel for them, enable yourself to empathise. This does not necessarily mean you must donate them money, yet do what you feel is right when you recognise them. Recognising them is enough to warm your heart and do your part. Pray. Feel. Smile. Smiling at them is already a step towards being a better person. It is undeniable that "a smile goes a long way". Yet again, such a guileless gesture can genuinely make you feel fabulous, so why aren't more of us smiling at each other?!

   Yield in serendipitous acts of kindness by caring for strangers and curing the wickedness. Ignite your delight without any fright, just smile and feel a steady flow emit through your body of being at ease with yourself- that is joy.

Take a photo – mindfully and meticulously

Nowadays when we are happy, we tend to want to share the feeling via social media. That is fine. We are blessed with the extensive and exhausting forms of connection to keep up with memories, but it can all get a bit too much. Sometimes it can heavy our hearts with the wish for approval of others rather than being present and taking photos purely for memory's sake. We get lost in social media, encouraging us to post to our heart's content. However, is our content really at the heart of it all? Is our photo-taking making our heart content?

Our automatic reaction to amusing moments and beautiful milieu urge us to "take a selfie", stream a live video or pose for the perfect pic. Is this really who we have become? Selfless selfie addicts who only want to venture somewhere for a photo to plaster on social media. Yup. Wasting precious time on capturing THE sublime shot that you have in mind. Practising poses until the actual setting of the photo fades away into the distance. Aiming to become Instagram famous for modelling in pretty places... the list goes on as the pressure multiplies and panic rises.

   With vanity embedded in the centre of it all, taking photos has turned us into self-absorbed junkies. Anxious ridden waves take over as one rides the motions of validation from others, about to drown in self-remorse because the vast ocean of social media makes the present photo world a competition… of concern. The concern here lies in the fact that we are a society with an ideology of "living our best life has never been easier".

   Social media has allowed for photos to overtake and egocentricity to undertake through the act of a click. Photos pop up here, there and everywhere. There have never been so many possibilities when it comes to capturing the moment, that it has made us shoot for entirely the wrong reasons. Setting intentions to take a nice photo is not healthy when a certain amount of likes or winning popularity is the prime goal.

These are full of anxious ridden feelings that feed off your doubts, fears and jealousies. The essence is lost when taking photos takes you away from living the experience. We end up looking at life through another lens. We look at life through another mind. We look at life through a camera to convince people we are living the best life. Why should other people play any practical role in the rating of your life? Your life is yours and so you should live it without the reliance of having to connect and capture constantly, at a rate that rages your self-confidence.

Share but do not compare. Look but do not degrade. Snap but do not care too much. Snap out of it. Hear your inner thoughts when snapping and be aware that you are taking photos for you, and not for others, there's a difference. You have nothing to prove, nothing to live up to. When taking photos becomes more of a fight for your frame of mind to prove itself to other people, then danger occurs. Being so taken away by the limiting factors of likes and followers is something that is in full flow right now and something that needs to stop.

Assert yourself. Bring yourself back to you and recognise that you are the truth. Affirm your idea for taking a photo, before unconsciously committing to blasting your camera out at every given opportunity taking away the essence of capturing the moment. This will only distance you to yourself and others that are around you. Make an effort. You are here and humbled to be in the presence of loved ones, lovely landscapes and the rest, so before spending half an hour for that one photo you have your hopes set on, ask yourself the five W's:

Why are you taking it? What is it that attracts you? Who am I taking it for? How do I want this photo to look compared to what it already is? Where is my motive lying or shining in the photo?

Start noticing the reasons that rival your conscience when snapping relentlessly and see how taking out your phone straight away shows a lot about your priorities. Reset, recharge, regain worth by switching off obscene priorities. Set them straight because snapping away is about savouring the moment and not wasting it away... Spend your time taking photos for the right reason. Look through your lens with intention, thought and care. Appreciate everything for what it is before unconsciously reaching for your phone to take a photo. One photo says many words, where too many photos don't say much.

Either way, we aim to capture events quickly because that is what our smart access phone cameras have made us become. Do we even sit still for a minute to make the most of what nature has to offer any more? In this sad time of selfie addicts, nature is still there. It is compliant in its stillness and serenity, but we take it for granted now more than ever. It's hard, I know. We all do it. We are all culprits in the camera world where the most impressive places comprise of people taking pics and disappearing once the ultimate shot has been achieved. It is great to take photos, don't get me wrong. Memories are more magical than anything. Yet, what is the reason you go out into nature or explore? Reconnect with yourself? Disconnect with the world? Allow yourself to truly take your phone out for the right reason, right time and you will see how you will start to feel fine.

Rewild yourself

Interacting with nature is important and it is effortless to rewild yourself. It is a remedy to unwind and right to rewild. Being around nature can simply involve sitting by the river or being at the beach, either way, the conscious immersion of oneself in nature restores hope and revives joy without any force involved. Interacting with nature is an individual act of self-care.

The special part about employing the natural world to nurture ourselves is the fact that every one of us can find our own novel way to wander with the creation and let go of our woes. Be it a picnic at the park or surfing at the beach, we all have our ideal perks of infusing ourselves in our environment that provide us with an irrefutable impression of peace. Rewilding yourself is about waking up to realise just how lucky one is to be encompassed by energising landscape, seascape or simply the tweeting of birds in trees. Taking time to tantalise your senses with scenery is free and makes one feel freer, where the impression of belonging and connection occurs.

Ever see the way children dig right into sand or dirt? The way kids get stuck into the sand and get creative without caring about the dirt? Why not do it? simply sticking your fingers into the soil or a plant, it has been proven that your mood will be enhanced and ignited with a peaceful state of mind as you forget the foes of daily life. Crazy, right? Just as trees have their magical power, dirt does too. The soil sings to your heart and boosts your immune system, making gardening nourishing in every way possible.

Not only are you planting, but enriching yourself simply by poking and prodding around participating in an act of self-care. Gardening is about growing. You get to grow your produce, as well as grow in harmony with oneself. Gardening is an act of love. It promotes longevity through its ability to sink stress and boost heart health. As you physically plant seeds and continue to water them, the seeds of love are planted within you and watered with your self-care.

Gardening is a self healer. Taking time to yourself will bring self-esteem to the surface and enable it to shine bright through the sense of accomplishment. Gardening is about getting dirty (not dirty in that sense, shh). You have to get stuck in and lose all prospect of fighting with the muck and make the most of it. Let go. As you seed and see plants blossom, so will your confidence and kindness. Gardening is an all-round positive act of self-love and guarantees peace, love and joy to sprout up all over the place.

After gardening comes cooking! Once you rewild yourself within your territory of harvesting home-grown food, cooking will become more fun than ever. Cooking is known to have an abundant amount of attributes in raising one's confidence, mood and enthusiasm. It is a method to be enjoyed and enlightened by, a mindful practice that involves concentration and creation skills to thrive.

Rewilding yourself concerns taking time out in nature with the sole intention to just be. We struggle with the term "to be" in our crazy capitalist society these days because we are driven by the wrong reasons and do not make ourselves the main character in our film – life. Look and listen to what is around you, so that harmony can be achieved through purely being around creation. According to the World Economic Forum, 2009 the Finns, as the happiest country in the world, revealed that harmony with nature and oneself is the secret to their happiness. That says it all.

Connection

Connection is key:

- To nature
- Social connection/ bonds
- Shaped by our social environment
- So many identities are available for us to feel
- Community & change
- Channelling your energy in the right way and the peace will be manifested
- You are a part of something: you are not determined by disorders
- When you realise we are all the same, you realise there is nothing more than connecting with one another
- Connecting and communicating brings a collective feeling
- Our world waves away connection and distances us all.
- Looking for forms of connection to feel whole.

What is connecting?

Connection is key to humankind. Connection is the constitution of incomparable companionships that preserve us as happy and healthy human beings. Connection is like the substance that sustains us to feel accepted, loved and cared for and is sought through family ties, friendships and relationships. Be it a warm embrace or simple chat, connections deliver compassion, bringing us together for us to feel a part of something special, something shared, something bigger.

Endeavour in everyday connection and a sense of inner peace will season your soul. Each connection is unique, as every person is. Each association enriches us differently. It is almost impossible for every attraction force formed to be put into words due to its authenticity, dependent on establishment or friend circles for example. A connection can be evoked in a sudden, brief exchange or it can be created over time.

Being connected is a feeling induced by the reliance on a social bond between two people or more. In our modern-day era of technology, a connection is instant and readily available at our fingertips, making bonds with mankind more accomplish-able through a screen rather than with sight. We are wired in a way where connecting is compulsory for our development, determination and drive. Being in the presence of other people has input in our actions or thought flow and rhythm. We thrive off connection because sharing news with others gives us a sense of reality, putting things into perspective.

Getting together provides a sense of belonging, growing together brings a higher sense of being. We flourish off connections because we react positively when shown care and compassion, strengthening us. Similarly, we can easily lose touch with ourselves if not shown springs of affection. Healthy connections heal our souls and soothe our minds. We crave contact to guarantee the feeling of being wanted. We need communication to take away the feeling of loneliness.

The pit of loneliness stems from our natural need to be nurtured and cared for, whereas the kit of happiness solicitudes connection to ignite a collective feeling of hope.

All in all, we are humankind, meaning we must interact through kindness and compassion to prosper to our full capacity in life. Sharing, caring, loving, the list goes on... are the branches that stem from the tree of connection. Let us find out how community and coming together may be the solution to the epidemic of loneliness.

How to connect and not control

Nothing is ever enough, we are never satisfied. Our current capitalist civilisation is torn up because of the fight for control and loss of connection. Some do not realise that it is our responsibility to club together and create a community with connection as the main component to convey the spirit of humanity in our world crisis. We must get back to basics and rediscover how the quality of union creates a feeling of wished-for wholeness while evoking a charge of change within societies.

Unfortunately, the mistreatment of connection with modern-day dating, fast ending friendships and broken families all contribute to us squandering over the worth and duration of relationships.

Mismanaging ourselves within relations by prioritising certain people and discerning others may lead to torment. Other times, some ties are harder to maintain than others, making us question "why" or "what is the point", wondering whether such relations are real or fake. There are a myriad of miscellaneous bonds that bewilder us, but can also teach us a lot as a person about what we want and deserve out of them. If some ties are harder to grip or hold on to, it is best to let go. If others are worth the fight because of the love that lights up, it is best to keep going. Each connection can offer us boundless teachings on who we are and who we want to be, it is all about your mentality. Becoming aware of what is good or what is bad for you is the first step in fabricating firm relations.

Let us rewind and reconcile organic connections for true change to come about.

It is in our nature to connect...

In the beginning, we were created to connect and communicate. No matter how you see it we are put on the earth to procreate. The meaning of association can be comprehended from our simplest form of being that makes us who we are. Every one of us is made of cells that are assigned to other cells to collaborate with, a never-ending process predetermined by our body, not our mind. This collaboration concerns an uninterrupted interaction that is simultaneously occurring without our conscious consent, proving that it is natural for us to connect and grow; rightly shown to us by our beautiful body.

Our biological matter and maintenance teach us that interaction is embedded within us, it is a part of us and continues creation. Adapting that consistent interaction into daily life and those around us is where some stumble upon because bonding with others is something that is taught, put into practice and experienced.

Therefore, childhood has a strong influence on the way we connect and can neglect or perfect our mannerisms and attitude. As a child we learn how to communicate, causing it to be the bedrock of development. It is fair to say that our social environment shapes us to be the person that we are because as humans we all have a basic need to associate and surround ourselves with people that provide the biological drive of connection. From a young age, relations can determine or deter our route of kinship in the future, as it affects factors that we take into account such as trust. We are formed to function off of connection because isolation insists on detachment to others to develop.

A healthy upbringing consists of a social circle of love, kindness and affection. For example, if a child is not regularly physically embraced by a warm hug or a tender kiss, then the consequences can be fatal where the absence of connection can take a massive toll on how to naturally form connections in the future. However, do not dismay, a child without love can still learn to love when older. That is the best thing about us; we thrive off each other's kindness and compassion. There is no end in learning love and creating connections.

Reflect, rewind and revive

For the first time, it has been noted that children are finding their form of attachment through friendships rather than their parents. In other words, the studies show that peers are taking over in radically contributing to each other's upbringing. This growing crisis amongst children losing their emotional and physical support from the people who are supposed to be raising them finds another procedure of attachment to pop up in the equation: technology.

It is rupturing into the realms of real connection and reversing our natural knowledge to interconnect into social anxieties. Parents must intervene. Take control of connecting with your young ones from a young age and don't let it be up to friends to form their sense of kindness and love.

We must teach our young future that phones are not the main device to communicate with, but how can we do this if all of us are more or less mind-boggled by our mobiles and find companionship in them? It is not just children that we should be concerned about, it is all of us.

We are all contributing to this epidemic of phones ruining our relationships where we are suffering from the first-ever epidemic of loneliness on a world-scale. There has been a dramatic change in culture because the shift of real-life connections has now been taken over by technological temptations where means of communication online are first in line. The power dynamic of technology is beyond our imagination, but because of who we are, we cannot hesitate or withhold its progress. Our addiction to phones is getting out of control, increasing social distress and depression to make decisions for us.

Yes, we are involved with each other but on a

virtual level rather than an absolute level with a proper physical presence. We have to accept that everyone is stuck to their screens, condemning our spirits to shed and turning us into robots as the struggle to reach out and truly connect with people becomes harder because our phones have become barriers and our private caretakers. This is proven through the fact that we are having to be taught how to communicate in person where people suffer more from anxiety when interacting personally because they prefer the effortless conduct via a screen of some sort. This sort of social drive has become normalised.

We prefer the practicality of social platforms. However, it is only going to produce hostility towards real-time communication that we cannot escape unless we put our phones down. You take your phone out to check it – check it for what? Leave your phone in your bag and accept that you are unreachable when with someone or some people, shouldn't that be socially accepted rather than having our phone on the table 24/7?

The essence of conversations are being lost as we now can converse with two people at a time; one via our phones and the other in person. Multi-tasking or multi-talking is becoming the standard, where we are not giving our devoted attention to anyone, not even ourselves. We are suffering because of us, then we wonder why we are all lost and lonely... Real connections are becoming brief and rare to find. Linking up with people in person requires time, effort and attention (something that we all seem to lack these days) making real relationships harder to maintain and manage in the rigorous flow of life that we have chosen to unravel.

To regain authentic means of connection, we have to re-attach ourselves to the importance of real-time relations and re identify ourselves as a race that wants to go forward together through communication. Here and now. We all crave a sense of community, that's why there are so many marketing strategies to lure people in utilising tribal tactics to make you feel like a part of something more, but most of all, to feel worthy rather than just an average human being. We want to feel like we belong, we always have.

Human contact teaches us so much as a child to the point that if we were not shown how to sustain social bonds in our early years, then the craving for healthy connections is surely heightened as well as fractured. However, our desire to connect is not totally dependent on our upbringing - it comes from within. Since we are wired to mix, we can learn to channel our energy in the right way to configure connections and manifest peace and positivity within one another. Research suggests that when we converse and connect, beliefs of others flood through easier even if we are not consciously aware of it. Since the bonds we build affect our thoughts and outlook, engaging with the correct contacts is vital for our health and happiness.

If you do not collaborate with care then you can become fragile and favour other people's opinions over your own, or even end up dismissing your own on the way. Power and control can spread like fire if one engages with someone that sucks all the freedom out of you. It's OK to want other people to accept you, but you must have accepted yourself first for it to be acceptable.

False friends are found in every corner and can destroy you, especially if you lose sight of what is real.

Be aware of healthy and unhealthy connections

Fake friends are like fast fashion: hard to keep up with but easy to be pulled in by. A lot of people look for different designs to find out what fits them or does not suit their standards set, whereas others copy and conform to the social "norm" and end up feeling torn. Likewise, the same applies to friendships. Understandably so. Every one of us commits the act of seeking acceptance when building connections, it is only human. We all want to be accepted for who we are. Naturally so. It is harder to show your true colours at first sometimes because conducting yourself in your weird and wonderful way might lead to judgment or embarrassment. If you are so sure of who you are then this should not matter. People are going to judge no matter what, so isn't it best to be judged for who you are rather than the fake you. Just be you.

We ought to respect one another, but unfortunately, this is not the case. Primarily, the people you love the most are those who accept you in every way possible. So remember to have your wits about you when surrounding yourself with new people because false friendships and corrupt connections are fuelled by a surge of dominance and control that cause pain and perturbation. Pick and choose carefully, do not be misled by certain characters. Put yourself first.

God declared, "Bad company corrupts good character." (1 Corinthians 15:33) We ought to stay true to ourselves when creating connections. If not, we can get lost and become someone who we don't want to be based on those around us. If you see yourself changing around some people for the worst, then simply withdraw and see how you feel after a few weeks. Decide who makes you feel good and who makes you feel bad, it can be that manageable. If people are bringing you down – eliminate them. When people are lifting you – embrace them.

Make a list of people that lift your spirits and others that dampen them, reflect and meditate on it.

Immerse yourself into the power of connecting

At times, our aims endanger regulations of relationships and can cause heartbreak in hope of something that is an illusion of the mind, especially if high expectations are involved. When we associate ourselves with people, we must not base it upon preconceptions. How? Consider the other person's feelings as well as our own. Accept them for who they are, listen to what they have to say, look them in the eyes, learn from their being and feel fully immersed by their presence. If you aim to make connections purely based on the person's look, for example, that's where it goes tits up. Don't fuck yourself over just because you are vain. That doesn't mean shit.

Get to know someone with no exalted expectations that may compromise the to-be acquaintance. If you do so, then cheerfulness, charm and change can flood through the gates of getting to know someone for who they genuinely are.

Respect every relation for what it is. Each interaction is as unique as the person. Do not conform yourself to a "type of person". These days, with technology at the forefront, we have all become pretty cocky without really realising it! Allow everyone to be who they are by believing that goodness exists in all of us in different shapes and sizes. This may sometimes be harder to dig out of certain people than others because some people just suck (it's true, come on!), but even then it is possible to learn something from every interaction. You can learn that you don't want to be that selfish or egoistic from someone or you can learn to be kind and compassionate from another. Our intercommunications teach us a lot about ourselves.

We are shaped by a complex set of interconnected and internal factors set out by our emotional needs and intellectual requirements. In other words, we pick and choose out the people who are close to us based on shared likes, opinions and qualities. This complex set of factors also configures itself with the outer world and we are strained by society to be pessimistic, doubtful or judgmental about someone before even getting to know them. Seeing the best in people is one of the finest things a person can commit. Give everyone a chance to channel their energy and you will be able to recognise if it is an energy you wish to encircle yourself with or not.

Back to the aim of acceptance: once adopted and applied in life, the easier it will be to get along with people and develop prosperous relations. Put preconceptions aside and start to look at each person as a sibling because essentially that is what we all are. Dalai Lama recently re- insinuated the dire need for us to improve person-to-person contact by adopting a universal responsibility to acknowledge brotherhood and sisterhood to enhance human understanding, of which there is a growing need for.

"Unfortunately, such ideas have been cheated by selfishness. More than ever before, we witness today how ethics and noble principles are obscured by the

shadow of self-interest."

When participating in person-to-person contact, can you just focus on that person or those people you are surrounding yourself with? Try it out, see what it shows you. If we simply aim to take each other for the form that they are through listening lovingly, then we can salvage the real sense of connection that we have all put on hold to a certain degree. Immerse yourself into the moment. Listen. Look. Let yourself be in that person's presence completely.

Take away the prejudice to judge and permit yourself to trust.

Trust in connections. Feel the vibrations. When you establish a good intuitive, then the key to knowing who to trust will come naturally, even during initial encounters. When I meet someone for the first time and feel a good vibe instantly, then I know it is someone I should make an effort with and see if our friendship will flow or if a relationship will grow. Some people you will just know, with others, it may take time. Everything takes time. Travel and get to know many kinds of people, as well as yourself and friendship groups or it could just mean having to realise what you cherish in people that you love. Once we realise that we are all connected then change for the better will be round the corner. At the end of the day, connections are configured to create a sense of wholeness. They are there to empower us with purpose - something we are all looking for.

Feel complete through connections

Loneliness is what gets in the way of unity. One of the greatest challenges for us all is to feel complete. Due to the many identities and labels that are out there, a compelling urge exists for each one of us to rightly justify ourselves in society. We are steered to stay away from society's hidden truths so that we become cynical about connections as well as ourselves. In turn, our minds are being distorted through the disengagement of emotions and enrolment of political leaders, for example. Through this misconduct of detaching, dividing and distancing rather than reconnecting with our true selves, we become reliant on what other people think of us and concentrate on how we want people to perceive us as. Who cares? As long as you know who is important (as well as why) in your life, that is all that matters.

Who do you want to be and how can you be a better person through relating to others around you? Show compassion. Be there. Stay honest. The world waves away connection and welcomes corruption instead. That is modern-day life, full of brief banters and hasta pronto partners. We are misled through many modes of transgression. When you are more connected to what you want and who you are, this should not affect your companions.

The problem of current times is that it convinces us to feel imperfect and proposes ways in which the outer world will help us fill this gap. Not to say that the gap cannot be filled by fad ways of the world, yet it does not allow us to reach our state of happiness untouched by outer things. We have dismissed one of the most important things we are all here for - connection.

At the end of the day, we have all been put on this earth to procreate, clarifying that connection is a principal part of our composition. Our path to completeness does not have directions, nor does it entail a thread of things that must be completed or satisfied within our span of Life. However, one thing is for sure: interaction. We are taught from a very young age that one of the three things living organisms require to prosper is interaction. The connection is an essential part of our path, so why are we neglecting it?

Connections allow us to be the best us. When we seek organic, healthy and happy associations without expectations, we get to know each individual for the person that they are as well as allowing ourselves to be who we truly are. They teach us what we appreciate about people.

The little things that one only notices in serendipitous moments. The way that someone smiles, for example. It is up to us to sustain and share our knowledge so that we can thrive off one another, rather than put each other down. The more we look at one another for who they are without any trace of judgment, and appreciate them for THEM, the easier it will be to connect and care for each other. Look out for one another.

Our energy is charged through interacting and is dependent on close connections to feel like we are a part of something special and bigger. Interacting with one another allows us to understand each other, as well as get to know ourselves better. It is about putting yourself outside your comfort zone at times to know who you want to hang out with.

I have been lucky enough to connect with people all around the world, where I take something small and sweet from every person I meet. This empowers me to grow and show gratitude for passing cherished moments in the presence of each individual. I uncover something from everyone that teaches me to be a better person. Each person I meet, I make sure I manifest in all their imperfect perfections so that I can learn something new about them that can flow into my life. Listen. Listen to what people have to say and take it in your stride.

This way you will be able to appreciate people's perspectives. I realised if I truly endeavour to hear people and immerse myself into their mannerisms, attitudes and quirks, I am taken away by them. I am engrossed by people. I allow myself to absorb and mediate their characteristics so that I can fully be aware of what they are uttering. Understanding and acceptance will follow because listening without any biases or judgment present are one of the most humble and heartwarming things we can do for one another.

Online connection is a tricky one

We all look for forms of contact to feel whole and these days it is predominantly sought through screens. Nowadays, the meaning of connection is being thwarted by our conception of online communication. Social media has exploded. It has enabled us to all have a voice, which can be more endangering rather than empowering at times. We are lost in a world that guarantees exchange because of the immediate responses that are expected of every one of us when conversing online. When the impossible becomes possible, we only want more from each other, which sometimes is what breaks us apart instead of brings us together. When one can connect with anyone whenever, communicate with whoever, the feeling of connection is modified according to our expectations (or lack of). We can be whoever we want to be. We can connect with whoever tickles our fancy.

This feeling of connection can cause the craving for a real connection to fade away or be thwarted into the frustration of feelings. We cannot ignore it. The power of communication through technology has overwhelmed the majority of us, it gets too much. You end up feeling alone if you are always online. Sounds weird, but it is like that. Why so? Such connections do not give us the gladness of looking into someone's eyes and being present and living in the presence of people, not to mention the radio waves that are being transmitted into our brains, that we are too ignorant to take into consideration. We are delicate after all.

We cannot get enough of each other. We can now control the amount of connection we have with people over our technological devices. However, face time differs dramatically to real-time. You cannot control what you say when you are with someone, making it more real and relevant as well as passionate as turbulent. We get to edit the person we want to be and the voice that we represent through the plethora of social platforms that are available at our fingertips.

OK, so it is not always a negative aspect because we are now able to stay in touch with people that are close to our hearts but far from our homes. However, the notion of real connection may sometimes seem out of reach. Human relationships are precious and rich; they necessitate time and love where online connections simply require a tap and a click.

We are slowly but surely misleading ourselves on how relationships work, because texting and talking differ entirely. We are allowed to control ourselves when corresponding online whereas in person this is not possible. We can be unclear online whereas in person we must explain ourselves. We can be who we want to be, so **be a good person**. We want to spend time with machines now more than ever because they make us feel like we are listened to.

Our relationships with screens are making us all participate in an extraordinarily sad seizure of our time: disconnection. Online communication adds up to oblivion because it is not of the essence. Utilise the array of conversing online to brighten your day - a text goes a long way. Hearing someone's voice on a call can clarify one's mind. Seeing someone's face on a screen showers you with adoration. Enable yourself to communicate cunningly online, it is a great asset for us in this day and age. Our phones can work wonders if you want them to.

The feeling of wanting to be understood is deep within us all and this is what makes social media platforms so appealing. We feel like we are a part of something bigger because being alone is a void and something easily resolved through our fingertips. The constant association is shaping us and showing us the constant craving for attention everyone deep down desires, demands and delights in. Technology is proving to populations all over the world that staying connected is something that we all now expect in our modern-day and might even be taken for granted now.

 Yes, it keeps us together and is the common ground of understanding, however it is distancing us with the feeling of being fulfilled from face to face interaction. We cannot distinguish what is empathetic or not through the face of a screen (only through the use of symbols and emojis, of course!). Whereas being face to face, one can configure a true feeling of understanding. We expect more from technology and less from each other because it charms us into an illusory state of companionship where we are in control.

 We can call anyone but we can also cut off anyone at any given point. It is scary. However, we are not in control – phones are. They can change our frame of mind for the worse. We expect everything to be quick and concise because we can access anything we desire using a wire. Our fragile sense of self is being put at risk because of the feeling of loneliness with telecommunication. We are not giving people in real life a chance any more. Who have we become? Essentially, robots. We are controlled by the media, the government, by everyone around us. Bring back the unique identities that can eliminate these infidelities we have poisoned one another with. Get back to our roots and realise that online communication can bring a power that may bring us all together with a surge to save the planet. Join groups that guarantee an abundance of positive interaction. You can use technology for the greater good, go for it.

The following pages show you how to connect with compassion and care...

Cooking is caring

Set yourself specific slots during the week that fit your schedule to cook for yourself as well as other people. Invite friends over. There should be a period during the day that you find meaningful enough to leave your mobile aside, giving yourself and loved ones the time they deserve. For example, dinner time.

Cooking for each other is such a cultural and contagious way to ignite a kindred spirit of love and gratitude. Every culture begets its ornate fashion for cooking up a storm. It is a harmonious model of bringing people together, a time to sit back and enjoy what has been gladly made for you. It is something so simple but special. Although cooking and dining take time (of which we are limited nowadays), time can always be found for food. Food is life. Feeding is fulfilling. Most of all, sharing is caring. When we combine the fulfilment of an essential survival need as a shared experience, one can fully come to appreciate the power of connection by coming together.

Eating together pleasures being alive in its rawest form. It is necessary to take time out so that you can gather, engage and recharge through people's presence and subsistence, both making you feel complete - mentally and physically in this case!

Look into people's eyes

I don't mean it creepily! Rather, in a gentle, kind and respectful manner of communication, eye contact is crucial. Fostering a childlike demeanour can help. For example, when a kid embraces you for no particular reason or gives you a piece of their cake... take this innocent and naive state of sweetness on and look into someone's eyes when they talk to you.

It makes the moment so much more intimate and interesting, trust me. Don't be scared. Eye contact shows empathy and sympathy - something we cannot get enough of and direly call for these days as our screens get more eye time than anyone else! During a conversation, eye contact is vital to keep engagement flowing. We have short attention spans due to technology overriding our deep communication skills, so disconnect and connect with those around you.

We are programmed to respond to faces and feel each other. The physical presence of people is powerful, so aim to be grateful and aware through a magical stare.

Learn from your pets example

From bees to dogs, all animals rely on communication to get by. The same goes for us. Bees rely on communication to decode information and get things done, busying around making their sound.

Dogs converse with body language so that we know what is wrong with them. This network of social support is evident through every creature on earth. We all NEED to communicate to co-exist and attempt to live together in harmony. The best thing about it is that it promotes survival in nature. When finding social stability and support with one another, the brain rewards us. The happy chemical oxytocin is released when finding safety and alarms you with cortisol when in danger.

Thus, our brains are wired so that we may be in equanimity with one another, rather than in conflict. Learn from your pets openness with other animals (ok, don't go licking bumholes!) and take on tolerance and responsiveness towards others.

Music is magic

Go to concerts, open airs, karaokes, band nights with people. It is a marvellous manner of mixing with others and letting loose. Music helps you be. Let go and listen. Look at the people you are with, feel comfortable to not have to control anything at that moment.

You are all bonding over a shared like in music, making magic through the union of appreciation. Music is like a mutual friend. Find the same interests with people and play with it, roll with it and allow it to strengthen your bond. It brings a passionate fire of becoming enraptured and enthusiastic together in light. Use music to make everlasting connections.

Join new groups and get socialising

Some of us are introverts, others extroverts. Millicent Fawcett, the woman who fought for women's right to vote says "Courage calls to courage everywhere". In this context, we must encourage ourselves to make the effort in meeting new people. Don't be afraid. Everyone has been in the same boat as you before.

Today, our options are endless. Thanks to the internet, we have a great resource to meet up sites where we can socialise, network and get together with people we might not know... yet. Take a chance. It will further your independence and confidence in yourself. I found that as a solo adventurer meeting with fellow fans of life to discover new places was something so extraordinary, I never felt more alive. Strangers in the same position ready to explore together - what better way to connect?! Everybody begins as strangers, don't forget that.

Educate one another

To salvage the sense of real connection, it is our responsibility to educate the youth to yearn for interaction in real life and harness the hope that communication will bring change. Considering the majority of teenagers view their phones as key in their social life where nearly half of US teens say their social life would not exist without their phones. What an utter shame in my opinion... it should shake us to preach about the prioritising real-time communication and its benefits. The speed of social media has highlighted the focus of well-being and how we can use our platforms to better the world instead. The issue of mental health has a lot to do with social media, but it also has to do with the lack of physical interaction: communication, understanding and spreading love only comes through authentic connection. Simply by being in people's presence enables an enormous feeling of being understood to seep through. Teach, preach and beseech!

Karma Yoga

All of the above are acts of kindness. Acts to compel connection to occur in an organic condition. They could also be considered actions from the heart, which can be connected to Karma Yoga. For those yet-to-be yogis (yes, you are going to convert yogi too), there are three "types" of yoga recorded in the Bhagavad-Gita, this being one of them. It is known as yoga for action.

The Hinduism strategy of existence sites the requirement to reach a selfless state with God and the order of the world in mind. This self-transformation is achieved by always taking others into account by spreading compassion and contentment.

"By nourishing one another you assure the well-being of all" (Bhagavad-Gita, ch. 3, The Yoga of Action).

Ok, so that was simplified a lot, but this method may include cleaning, cooking and caring for one another. Be good to others and you will be blessed back. It is like the "karma" everyone throws around these days; give out good energy and you will receive your portion of positivity in return.

When you have the greater good of the people in mind, then you will always live true to your heart in avoidance of sinful acts. Of course, as humans, we cannot be completely "pure" but what I love about this teaching, also echoed in Buddhism, is that it is about stimulating a controlled engagement with one another. How? Through wisdom, desireless actions and good intentions are set for us to bond with each other to the best of our ability. Live in harmony. Withstand evil desires and expand in earthly desires to heal with hope through creating healthy connections.

The knowledge is within you

The knowledge already exists within every one of us. It is up to us to seek out the light and find what feels right. We have to access this knowledge through each other, so we can serve the function of humankind as a whole by being kind humans. It is our responsibility to club together, create wholeness through creativity and change.

One of our greatest strengths is sending signals of understanding, however, we take selfishness and deconstruct it into egoism with no room to care about others. Legitimising rugged individualism is about finding common ground with each other, it is our time to wake up and realise our potential. It is about you, but most importantly, it is about your place in this world as a tool for change.

Find meaning. We must realise we are all equal. We are all humans, made of cells assigned to collaborate to live and thrive off one another. Connecting and communicating brings a collective feeling, a higher ground that has the endowment to do anything and everything. Connect wisely and communicate effectively.

Why connection will bring change…

Life uses people as lessons to ignite transformation in each other and realise true potential. We live for connections. Everyone is seeking a sense of community, one way or another. Be it in a club, a church or a gym, contact is the ultimate way to go about change. We all crave interaction because we want to feel worthy, accepted and cherished.

This connection is now forged online for us all to want to be a part of, where we are suffering from a global epidemic of loneliness spurred on by technological devices and platforms that plunder our daily life into being submerged inside. There is no need to roam and relate with others outside now. Loneliness is a problem of civilization. We are being convinced that the cure is not a real connection but online deals, as well as consumerism with money being made.

Let us reunite in re-connecting with one another to make positive changes in cheery ways. For example, the feeling of reuniting with loved ones is incomparable. It is special, seasonal and sweet. Being with people that you can truly be yourself with is unique because of the joy and love it showers you with. Surround yourself with people that accept and adore you for who you are. Criticism can be banished and courage can blossom within you. When you identify that loved ones accept you for who you are, confidence will heighten and willingness to participate in loving yourself will grow. Love conquers all. It knows no limits. Start to realise who and what matters around you by allowing love to be the answer. Start to foster togetherness to unify and create upbeat moods for everyone to be a part of.

CONNECTION IS THE ANSWER!

There are an abundant amount of people that are currently suffering in our world. I don't mean from external factors that are not in our control, yet features that are driven by us and, thus can be deterred by us. We are the catalyst of loneliness. Loneliness is a result of our decisions (up to a certain extent). Loneliness is conceived through the handling of technology, for example. 1 in 6 kids now have an attention deficit, suicide rates are soaring in young men and anxiety disorders heighten with teenage years. Isn't that enough to want to make a change and do your part in participating with love in your heart?

According to the World Forum, 4% of the global population suffers from an anxiety disorder. There are a diversity of diseases that we are suffering from, there is no denying it. With Social Anxiety Disorder ranking 3rd in the world, we cannot ignore it. We wonder why so many health issues are arising when it is quite plain and simple. Our decisions are our plagues. Caused by the environment, lifestyle and technology, we have become an organ of disease due to the epidemic of capitalism, chemicals and consumerism.

A significant number of kids are now getting brain tumours due to the potential exposure of chemicals and radio waves, but we do not want to admit to it. We have become sheltered, lonely and laden with problems, pushed to believe we cannot heal on our own, so turn to capitalist ways of consuming and end up decreasing all the while.

Connecting can solve this problem. Communication can strengthen us. I am sure of it. Essentially we all crave to communicate and connect, it is within our best interest. Why aren't we using it to heal rather than destroy and disrupt? Healthy interactions are important for our wellbeing. We live longer when we make strong bonds. We laugh for longer when we encircle ourselves with salubrious relations. We learn to be selfless and season others with our care and compassion rather than succumb to selfish acts. Relationships realise our true colours and potential because they are unique.

Studies prove the significance of serving each other
When a study was carried out with senior patients close to death, they were asked what they regretted in life. Many life lessons were pointed out. With youth fading, death looming, regrets arising, key

ingredients to a happy life rise to the top. Guess what the star of the show was? Relationships. You see, relationships hold more value than anything we can ever imagine or crave. Achievements, success and wealth are all driven by our need to excel and propel into a competitive world, whereas actions are priceless, precious. Relationships stick with you forever.

You will never forget the way a person makes you feel, resonating with your essence and realising your experience. In the end, all we have is love. It all comes down to love. When we are near to death, we realise the entire worth of golden relationships that have shaped and shaded us through the bad times and the good because connections consolidate the meaning to live.

"Love one another deeply, from the heart." 1 Peter 1:22

Don't be scared to love. I know, it can cause heartbreak and deep sorrow if breached. However, it is better to be loving than fearful to show your love, because you will always receive it back if you reveal it with righteousness. You do not have to search for the correct people to socialise with, they will come to you if you show a willingness to be of worth and attract your tribe. Be yourself and people will follow, it is about fitting in with those who genuinely accept you for who you are. Associate with people who share the same interests, have the same morals, laugh at the same jokes.

It is about being able to laugh at the silliest of things without being embarrassed and being still and sincere in serious times. Find comfort in connections. Go with your flow and you will know. It is OK to impress, but it is better to BE impressed. Acquire the knowledge of what attributes fit your style or what quirks fit your weirdness. Your attraction force will vibrate with acquaintances and you can decide if you want to surround yourselves with them or not. Do you feel uplifted with them? Is it easy and conversation flows? Some questions to put forth are ideal in realising who fits your flow. Comfort, understanding and acceptance are key in holding meaningful relationships. Your social crowd will accept you, even enhance you because they understand what makes you special and significant.

Start to accept, follow to appreciate, aim to amplify.

How can we change our perspective?

It is simple really. Set yourself specific times during the day that you find precious and meaningful to leave your mobile aside and give yourself and loved ones the time they deserve. For example, dinner time. Cooking for each other is such a cultural and contagious way to ignite love, kindness and gratitude amongst a number of lively beings. In every culture, cooking is something that brings people together in good spirits. Take time to sit back and enjoy what has been made by your own hands – it is something so humbling and joyous, yet something so simple. It, however, takes time and this is what we lack these days. Yet it is necessary to take such time out so that you can gather and engage with the people that make you feel like you.

Look into people's eyes. I don't mean it creepily!

Rather, in a gentle, kind and respectful mode of communication. Adopting a childlike manner may help, when a kid embraces you for no particular reason or gives you a piece of their cake just because, take the innocent and naive state on and look into someone's eyes when they talk to you. It makes the moment so much more intimate and respectful. Communication by eye contact shows empathy and sympathy – something we cannot get enough of and direly require these days as our screens get more eye time than anyone else! During a conversation, eye contact is vital to keep the engagement flowing and interest going. We have short attention spans due to technology overriding our deep communication skills that everyone has.

Guess what? Hope still survives because we are programmed to respond to faces and feel each other. Stop being smitten with technology and look into people's eyes, incur a sense of curiosity and keenness when meeting people. Find community, connect to nature, co-create with nature, etc.

To conclude...

The speed of social media has highlighted that we must focus on our well-being and utilise our platforms to better the world. The issue of mental health has to do with the lack of physical interaction: communication, understanding and spreading love only come through connection. Simply by being in people's presence enables an enormous feeling of being understood. The physical presence of people is important.

To salvage the sense of real connection we need to however educate our youth to yearn for interaction in real life and harness the hope that communication will bring change. In the end, it all comes down to love and relationships. Nothing else matters when you are on your deathbed, so start thinking like that. Life for relations.

We live in a busy world these days. And the pressures and demands of work, city life and trying to raise a family can take its toll on some golden relationships. Take time to realise who is important and import innate love.

Solitude

Henry David Thoreau: 'I never found the companion that was so companionable as solitude.'

What is solitude?

Solitude is a companion. Solitude is a glowing act of self-love. Solitude is a gratifying deed of self-care, caressing your will to be alone, at home. Everyone is responsible for spending time on their own in a healthy, happy and honourable manner, to replenish and rekindle the strength. Become satisfied with oneself. No added extras. You can rely on solitude to restore and revive, so much so it could even be the soundest start to truly get to know and love yourself with all your heart. The hope of the world lives within you.

Solitude acts as a step in making one realise how our pots of magic preponderate inside. Why so? It is empowering because joy is found in taking time to oneself to reflect, reinvigorate and revitalise one's perspective. Solitude is a subjective state of mind that involves being by yourself and manifesting in contentment with your own company. Loneliness, on the other hand, triggers feelings of isolation that hold one back from feeling any hint of happiness, instead bounding you to sink deeper into the low level of self-loathing rather than reach out for self-love.

Retire from being a skelf and rewire to your senses, through finding peace in solitude. Unearth a creative outlet or source of energy that makes you feel good without any outside influence. Loneliness concludes with the withdrawal of love, whereas solitariness concurs with welcoming love.

Imagine solitude as a mobile. Now, envision your mobile and how many times you must charge it during the day as you check it every hour or more. Basically, the more you are on your phone the more battery power it loses. Sometimes your phone can overheat when floods of messages and calls come through, or it starts to malfunction if too many apps are in use at the same time. Just like your trustee companion, you can also feel overloaded by work, relationships and constant communication that we all partake in.

As the battery life of our phone dwindles, so does our energy. It diminishes amid people and daily life as we encounter irrational thoughts and swamp ourselves with social events or burn ourselves out with work meetings. We must recharge. We are required to regain stability and relight our spirit as well.

Apply the same sense of charging your phone to yourself! The only way is to take time out for yourself. As individuals, it is vital in whichever way chosen to do so. However, a lot of people struggle these days with the concept of "being alone". Understandably so, considering that we are all bombarded in some way or other by the modern methods of development demanding us to keep up with the coming and going… then letting go of ourselves in the equation.

It seems that the importance of solitude is shrugged off some times at present because of how socially and successful our society urges us to constantly be concerned about. Care about yourself. Forget about the rest. It is now more than ever that we should take a step back and realise how exactly the execution of solitude is essential for not only health and well-being but survival in such an upside-down world.

Loneliness and Solitude are not the Same

Loneliness and solitude should not be mistaken for one another. Solitude is a positive play pro-actively sought out by one's yearning to reset, recharge, revitalise in self-love leading to fulfilment. Solitude has the power to elate us because we must enjoy our own company to fully find peace, joy and love within as well as around us. It is the state of actively accepting oneself, harnessing an awareness that sparks the quality of individuality and creativity to manifest within. It is permitting yourself to feel worthy.

It is something we willingly choose to do for our spirits to be restored. Loneliness, however, is something that we do not choose to experience because it is a grappling emotion that succeeds in tearing any piece of positivity into pieces through the method of making us feel abandoned and unable to enjoy one's companionship in its finest form. Rather, it is exchanged for confinement because of the false belief injected into one's mind to suffer from desolation distancing one's access to finding a feeling of inner peace.

To enjoy spending time in one's presence may be perceived to some people as weird or sad, signalling defeat when swerving to socialise with others. Rather, it is a sign of strength. You don't feel like it, or you require the rest with yourself. It's OK. You are not required to live up to anyone's expectations other than you own. Nonetheless, hanging out with the wrong crowd can indeed be the loneliest state of affairs in the world.

A lack of knowledge on how, why, where and when to spend time in one's company has caused the extreme epidemic of loneliness to rise. This is chiefly due to the effects of technology, where it is easier to feel lonely when confronting your actuality in exchange for aimlessly flicking through the array of social platforms on offer. Compare, compare despair.

Most of us seek out the company through a screen that strikes stress-induced emotions due to its capacity to baffle and bewilder our brains into thinking that we are alone, unimportant and maybe even left behind. Being in sync with our phones frazzle the willingness to be wary of solitude and its importance because we are so engrossed by others rather than observant to ourselves. Instead, the reliance on technological devices invites stress to seep through the screen sanctioning the goal of being by oneself something strange and scary. So why are we all in some way or other addicted to our phones?

Boredom. Loneliness. Gratification. The list goes on. Write a list as to why you think you rely on your phone and then look at how you could convert this to rely upon yourself.

Being alone is OK. It is so much more than OK. It is wonderful. It is a luxury. It is influential in coming to terms with being comfortable in one's skin. It is an achievement in itself due to forgetting about others and focusing on your one and only self. That is all that matters. You are all that matters. Unfortunately, studies show that young adults suffer the most from loneliness in comparison to the older generations these days, not to mention the plethora of mental health issues that have heightened too. Surely this signals that technology must have a part to play in the catch 22 effect of our dark and deep dependence attached to the outstanding number of handy gadgets. It is taking us further away from what is real, so we must rectify it by seeking out certain approaches to amplify our self-esteem.

Take a step back and think of who you are without your trustee telephone for a second. You are an instrument of love. You have a powerful potential ready to be awakened within you. We are a whole entity, every one of us should bestow the knowledge to be on our own and be fine with it. Why? Think of solitude as a holiday for your soul to recuperate so that you may be a brighter and happier being reflected in your attitude towards others and mirrored in your actions.

This vacation is something that should also be booked in advance and be seen as a necessity. There is no better way to refresh your outlook and let go than taking a well deserved holiday. So why are we not realising that taking a break by ourselves also applies the same way?

We have been manufactured into machines by society's standards, directions and expectations. Our reliance on phones takes refuge in the misunderstanding of madness that is initiated if you try to be alone and are not used to it. They have not only become our best friends but also another version of ourselves. Mobiles are our companions, as well as all the other appliances!

They see us through pretty much everything, in essence becoming a part of our persona through its abundant knowledge stored about us. We pretty much provide our phones with all our details as a backup, only then resulting in us to back up and feel shut out. The reliance on our phones is what we must zoom in on to zoom out of loneliness and focus on ourselves.

  We are allowed to be on our own. Furthermore, it is great to get to know yourself without a screen to surrender to. Allow yourself to take time to yourself. Get to know yourself. Solitude is bliss. Something that seems to be mistaken for being lonely these days should not be squandered but embraced. Ensure that there is a part of the day that you do not have your phone in your pocket or on your person. Free tech-time.

  Make one day of the week where you come home from work or time of day you put it away. Stick to it. Make it a habit. Put it to the side and participate in acts of self-love, such as drawing or writing, yoga or meditation.

  These acts of self-love distract us from the fad and

attach us to the present moment of letting go and leaving woe.

We must take the time of day to concur with our current emotions and come up with self-love potions. You are the one that discovers your remedy to be solitary.

Withdraw from what is around you and draw within you get a better picture of the person you want to be, take a step closer to feel free. The world is constantly changing and it is hard for us to keep up, where some feel the need to stay in the loop.

How do you feel? Are you trying to keep up with everything because everyone else does or because it makes YOU feel good?

It is up to us to take time, nobody else can commit a mime. It is up to us to find what feels good- nobody is going to tell you how. Listen to your heart and take part. Take part in looking out for yourself. This is the start and it is considered an art.

The art of soaking up the beautiful and brilliant benefits of solitude.

How?

Take time out.

The problem hovering over our heads these days is that time seems to be more limited because of all the options available to do in all the branches of life, blowing us one way and beating us the other. How is there enough time to do it all?!

The answer does not exist. It is up to you to decide what is worth your time and what is not.

This may overload us, forcing us to feel the strain and stretch. Yet it can also be turned into a positive because we are lucky enough to not run out of things to try out, tackle and take on. The possibilities in paths to choose are endless. For everyone. The career path is a prime example of how time seems to be so suddenly taken away from our fingertips as we fantasize over future goals. It involves a lot of dedication, determination and devotion in terms of "choosing" what career might best suit you and when it is "the one". But who knows? Nobody.

In the western world, finding a career path can be panicky because of the pressure piled on, plus society's drive to string us along to believe that the dream career defines and determines our worth. Think about it for a second. When meeting someone new, one of the first questions (if not the first) that pops to mind and uttered is "what do you do?". Of course, it is a central part of our lives so it mirrors who we are as a person... but only to a certain extent. A job does not define us. Work-life is not who we are. It is a part of our lives, but it does not declare our sole drive.

Our persona involves our aura, our interests, our passions, our family, our friends, our beliefs, our morals, our personality. These are the deeper and distinct factors that franchise your feelings for who you are.

So let's take a moment to mindfully rearticulate first-time questions to caring, considerate inquiries:

What do you do? - > What is your day-time job? What is your company's ethos? What are your passions? What is your job in the world? What is your mission in life?

How are you? - > How is everything going? How is life treating you? How do you feel these days?

How's work? - > How is your energy level at work? What kicks do you get out of your job? Any new projects you are involved in at the moment? What are your co-workers like?

Are you ok? - > Is anything the matter? Do you want to talk about it? What is missing right now?

Jobs, as well as relationships, correlate with your likes, dislikes, but they do not define you as a person.

Time is precious. The way we fill our time also is. It has the power to push us over the edge. It can keep us on our toes. It can be a source of serenity, replenishing us. Consequently, it is cunning in its control over us or we can be in control. Becoming more aware of right now is needed in our day and age to survive. This then cultivates a higher awareness. (But that's another story!)

Modify and manage your time so coping is a mechanism, not forced to fall under us. Work with time so it works for you. Sometimes it is tricky to designate that specific time of day to yourself because work and what not takes over. I also struggle with that, everyone does. No doubt about it (I can use doubt here shh) Take over your life by distinguishing what it is that is holding you back to reach your potential. Release. Regather your motives to spend quality time with yourself. Restore.

If you notice that you are putting too much energy into something that is not ideally serving you well; get rid. Raid your wardrobe of wishes and make them come true. You can always revise, repair and reshape your livelihood so that it suits your solitariness. If you are dedicating time to something that does not prove beneficial, reconsider what exactly makes you feel alive and allot that slot to yourself.

Let us begin...

Exercise is a good start

All you need is half an hour of exercise a day to fully reap the health benefits and recover a steadfast/stable state of mind. Start slowly and see what suits your body, mind and spirit. The wonderful thing about exercise is that it entails a wide variety of activities; the ample amount of choice signifies there is something to suit everyone's needs. The list is endless when it comes to the performance of improving and maintaining good health. Exercising alone elevates self-confidence because you are physically making a concerted effort of change in your daily routine by taking out time to stay in good physical and mental shape.

Find what fits you. Your motivation and dedication combined will become routine, natural, healing. Staying in tune with your wellbeing will be rewarding in many miraculous methods. Go with your rhythm and stick to it. Refrain from bringing yourself down and keep heading up. You can only get better.

Practice makes perfect. Forget about everyone else because exercise is a journey of personal growth (mentally and physically). Staying healthy and fit is something you do for you, not for anybody else. Thus, it will guide you to become stronger and stable so that you can achieve all the other things you yearn to do as well.

Exercise clears our mind in ways unimaginable because it releases endorphins and serotonin, unquestionably advances your ability to reach happiness and satisfaction. Exercise clears our minds like wiping a dirty surface does. Some call it the post-workout high that has a whole load of research behind it proving that exercise relieves pain and welcomes gain.

Hit the gym. Go for a run. Take a bike ride. Try out a dance class. Work out. Work out what is best for you. Decide what you think will empower you in ways that will allow you to feel fab and fit. A major workout winning people over is running. Many people have found running to play a successful part in their life, having converted their mentality and changed their life because of the marvellous feeling that running realises.

It makes sense if you think about it. The geographical element of moving away from the past and entering into what lies ahead of those haunting thoughts to be shed. You are physically running away from them. The state of running propels you in the direction in front of you: the future. The past is behind and all you have is the future to face. All you have is now. Such a sensation announces and asserts a very optimistic approach to become free of everything that might be holding you back. Get away from the worry. Go with the wind. Get your tunes on the go. Music has a massive role in further releasing stress when running. Plug in your music, prance with your beating pulse and welcome your magic movement.

The sense of achievement and aliveness is a bespoke feeling that any person can access through running plus the health benefits are HUGE.

As for me, I am not a huge fan of running. I don't run. I have tried it out, but it was not for me! The only time I have ever run is because I had to catch a bus or I was late for something… so I don't feel it is appropriate to continue advising on running. (Although on those occasions I was elated that I had proven to myself I could do it!) It was great. I did not think I could run to catch a bus, but then I did and the rush I felt after was exhilarating, to say the least.

Thus, I do see how getting your jog on is great and admire all the people that run by the river as I am sat there reading away absorbed in my world daydreaming into the distance. I have always aspired to be that person who went for a run every day but never managed it. Might be to do with laziness or simply that it doesn't suit me. I tried out jogging and it was great… but I much prefer walking. Walking is always a winner for me.

I feel like I can truly let go as my feet lead the way and the worries go away. It makes my mind drift into a delightful state of seeing the world for what it is by forgetting about the fads of my world that weary me, of which we all are wrapped up in one way or another. I find myself when I walk, especially in new places. It is a chance to get lost and leave what is not of worth behind to discover new paths not only physically but mentally as the mind wanders with you. Put a spring in your step and walk with might, managing to move you up and over the clouds that burden your mind.

Whatever form of exercise it is that you want to execute: give your all. Get yourself active, put yourself into it and prove yourself that you can do it.

If possible, exercise outside because finding euphoria in nature whilst working out is like taking vitamins for the soul. Getting fit does not always need to be in the gym, I find it frightening to see so many people surrounding me as if I have accidentally entered some sort of competition. You do you! Aerobic activities lead to a longer life. Cleaning and gardening count too! So what is holding you back? Start something new today.

Ok, you're now like *yeah, right where do you get this motivation from? or I don't have money for classes* So, you have trial classes for nearly everything. Make the most of it as you do with Netflix trial. Imagine a Netflix trial for three weeks for your body and mind to get back in shape - imagine how ripped you could be!

Travel alone

Liberate yourself by leaving and letting go. Explore. Go on an adventure. Discover new places. Wander the world in a way that opens your eyes to cultures and caresses your heart to tune in with different perspectives and people. Travel alone. Tantalize your curiosity in mysterious lands by choosing who you want to be, where you want to be. You can be anyone you desire, so choose wisely.

There is no better opportunity to become adjusted and in awe of your own company than putting yourself into a new territory, out of your comfort zone and with no choice but to discover and determine your own independence through taking decisions, making new connections and memories that all count towards the path of getting to know yourself. Not only are you proactively putting yourself out there, but you are urging yourself to dependently drive to a destination that will only make you progress as an individual. Water yourself well. When choosing to travel solo, a switch automatically turns on a current of curiosity and keenness to come to life. You have the choice to change your life for the better.

I do not see travelling alone as a bad thing at all; quite the contrary actually. I used to think travelling alone is cool when you are young, but then I met a Serbian lady on the U-Bahn in Berlin and she loved escaping solo. Even when you are older, if not, more importantly, you must take yourself out of your comfort zone and continue to discover new places. It is crucial for self-development.

5 personal development areas:
1) Opens your perspective
2) Opens you to new cultures
3) Opens you to new people
4) Opens you to a new cuisine
5) Opens your ears to hear languages

I believe it is a prime performance of self-love that leads to mastering your thoughts by digging deeper. You find out your feelings, acquire new interests in a way that nothing else can do so. Why? When you travel alone, you have no choice but to make decisions for yourself.

You have no alternative but to be bold and brave when unearthing a new reality. You find yourself in a real-life fantasy full of fresh faces and strange surroundings. You have a chance to champion in cultural awareness and combat the fear of the unknown. When I travel alone, I feel free. I feel exhilarated. Most of all, I feel me.

The moment I enter an airport is like turning the TV on, but with real people parading around you with different destinations and stories, it is truly fascinating (before even reaching your region of choice!). People-watching pounces at your ability to ponder and ignite inquisitiveness as realisation reigns in on your capacity to understand that you are a part of something so big and beautiful. The realisation that everyone is living a life as complex as you are: *sonder in its finest form. Self-realisation is a real insight when exploring alone.*

Taking a flight to an unfamiliar place with unknown faces curiously peering at you in every corner can bring in a self-realisation like no other. Catch your attention to enter into another world and see things for what they allow you to be aware of who you are too. Daily antiques don't challenge or confront your character as much as being in alien spaces. Not only the subject of self-realisation sets in, but the battle to be you sheds before your eyes because of the possibility of being whoever you want to be. Your mask is set aside as you arise in areas without familiar faces.

No remnants of the past linger around reminding you of what was. Instead, new foundations are found to remind you of what is. That is all that matters. The present moment and your mission. Marvel at the newness. The positive values of travelling assist you in further development.

The opportunities in opening yourself up to what is around you are perplexed and inspiring to your self-worth. Remember, life is a journey, not a destination (an overused quote I know). It is up to you to ride the journey and develop in destinations unknown.

The impact of returning is really when the realisation of how much you have changed sets in, as well as appreciation, gratitude and gladness for the life that you are living. Hygge springs to mind. (The feeling of cosiness, comfort and content evoked by simple comforts.)

Travelling alone is like opening a book without having read the blurb or being given a backstory: it is up to you to read and rave with your soul-searching appetite for what lies ahead.

"I think every woman should travel alone because it helps you grow and you also realise how much you are capable of." Aline

Try new things out

There is nothing better than adoring life for what it is- an endless amount of adventures on offer waiting for you to embrace. Positive and negative lessons look at you in the mirror every morning. It is up to you to reach out, reload or reverse in the ravings of daily life. They are out there in many shapes and forms ready for you to unravel yourself. From learning to loving, we are always trying new things out that change and chase us into complex channels of energy. Everything is made of energy- you can chase them according to what charges you. It's like trying out new batteries- some have a shorter time than others, you are the one that chooses to spend more time, money or effort in one for a longer life.

Adopt a curious mind and adhere to fresh beginnings, steering yourself away from unhealthy habits and driving towards hobbies that heat your happiness. It is true to abide by the saying that you never know you will like something until you try it out. You might have been pondering over the possibility of starting a new class of some sort that has been stashed away at the back of your mind, like that old book you got for a penny at the garage sale years ago, now a dust collector waiting for that day to be opened up.

Dig up your desires and unearth your yearnings to take centre stage in your mind by figuring out a way to make it possible. Don't mean to "quote" Nike but just do it.

Be it a dancing or cooking class inspired by hours of dedication to TV shows tickling your fancy, find out what it is that stirs your senses and try it out! Creativity is infectious. Take your religious viewings on Netflix every night as a sign to start something similar (of course, not the horror or crime dramas!). It may be something so out of the ordinary that has made you back up and let go…

Bring it back and forget about it being a dream in the distant land of "I'd love to do that one day". Those people who have dreams about taking on something that are so "not them" or concern the doubt of others are prime examples to extinguish your laziness and ignite your readiness. Sure- prove them wrong.

Yet don't do it purely based on another disbelief, but rather for yourself. That is what is most important: try something new out for YOU. We have to constantly be trying out new things if not discovering new places because it keeps hope. Hope, passion, inspiration are to follow.

These are the ingredients of a happy and wholesome life. Waking up with a reason is the "dream job", right? For this reason, more and more people are quitting their 9-5 and choosing to thrive. We are the rulers of our lives, although it may seem like a battle at times.

I have a huge list of things I have wanted to try out for ages, but have simply put them off due to life getting in the way. Don't let it. Life is for that exact reason. See how thrilled kids are enjoying new hobbies? We shouldn't stop while young, but yield in advancing our happiness forever. Putting yourself in strange situations sanctions growth and gratitude to rush through your body and mind. It invigorates you with new life. Learning is inspiring.

Living in Seville for the first time spurred me on to finally learn the sevillana dance before feria. Hands down, it was hard. Admittedly, I didn't learn the whole dance, but I did manage to make it to classes and succeeded in the first series. I was chuffed- I smashed it! The moment I got to show off my skills during feria made me be proud to achieve something new that I never thought I would have been able to do.

It is always good to go for something that revels with fear within because, in the end, you will feel brave and proud of your accomplishment (and rightly so). Distinguish what it is that might delight you but fright you and give it a go- you have nothing to lose, and everything to win.

Devote yourself to be disciplined

Discipline in dedicating time to yourself is like the love that binds two people together. Devotion, discipline, dedication, determination: the four D's that constitute the frame surrounding solitude. To firstly find the time for yourself, you must manage and make the most of time to suit your solo needs. Determine a certain schedule that involves specific times of the day where you will stop, switch off and start to see sweet serenity buried within your set solitary confinement. Open up to yourself. Sit still. Stand tall.

First and foremost, secure this time at the start or end of day and not just something you aspire to pioneer. The beginning and final hours of the day are your most empowering to devise a routine in realising your potential. It can concern a morning warm-up with writing, stretching, meditating, praying etc. Anything that thrives in setting good intentions is more attractive to adapt to.

Devotion and discipline come hand in hand. Set a time to be solo- it can be that simple to stick to. Ok, so we all don't have time at the minute, right? (I knew you were thinking this!) No matter how much we believe we are thrown off our feet for a time, rising and unwinding are committed by us all scattered out around the clock. Simply setting half an hour before bed or after waking could be a good starter to the solo structure.

Come up with a plan- write a list of targets that you specifically seek out of you-time. Or not. Decide in your mind and marry it with wonder. Setting yourself targets entertains solitude as a state of bettering yourself. However, setting targets also won't necessarily work if your heart isn't in it. Put it up on your mirror or toilet door - somewhere you are bound to gaze at during your day. A lot of the time we aim to be a better us at the start of a new year. Is it the perfect opportunity to feel fresh and fab? Not really, because your resolutions will run out of excitement in two or three months. That is why trying out something new should be incorporated. Every week or everyday, set yourself challenges if you want a change to happen.

You see, it is easy to enter into past patterns after January and forget about the intentions set supposedly for the whole year. In order to keep at it, your attention and willingness must be lavished. So choose something you feel like you won't get sick of, a hobby that will heal and hold you upwards on onwards.

Start simple. It could involve being alone and writing down your feelings (some may call it a journal or diary!). Now, dependent on what exactly you want to achieve within, think about a time of day that you thrive and feel most alive. My time is in the morning. If I don't have a morning by myself, then the rest of my day may just turn into mayhem. I specifically seek out to be solo at the break of dawn because it is the perfect time to set good intentions for the day ahead as well as manifest in positive energy to push me on throughout the day.

My mornings are like a little miraculous medicine working in my magic to be a better person every new day that I wake. I roll out of bed to make lemon water before doing a yoga practice (sometimes that consists of only 5-minute stretches if I am in a rush!), I then have a good breakfast (essential for my energy) whilst reading my bible and praying (crucial for my peaceful soul). Then, if time bids it, I will write in my diary what I want to achieve, which errands I have to run and notes about the daily duties that I aim to complete. Writing all this out helps my mind to be free of worry so that I can embrace the day for what it is.

My morning medicine is taking time to myself to wake up slowly and at ease, because I cannot rush into a day that I wish to pursue as a better person than yesterday. So what? My morning routine may not be the one for everyone and I don't do it every day because I am only human, as are you. That is also OK- accept and never put yourself down. Praise yourself for how far you are, and keep going. If you don't, nobody else will.

Daily devotion may be that key to unlock your unique character and its creativity. I aim to dedicate my morning to myself, but it is not always the case as said. You mess up, we all do. If you're too hard on yourself, you might be caught in the cobweb of goals- just remember your reason and let it light you up not light your ego up. Things happen and every day cannot go the way you want, this is something key to accept in the discipline of personal development as you can grapple with being disappointed in yourself some days. Learn to accept and be aware. Just accept every day as a new beginning and go from there. If not today, tomorrow is perfect too. Treat every day as a dare to do something you would have never done yesterday. This keeps your creativity alive.

Self-discipline is a practice within itself. It cannot be done in a day; it is driven by habitual dedication in developing ways to be delicate towards your character. Research suggests that a habit is only fabricated after 21 days, so let's say it takes a whole month of making something a habit that is performed on a daily occasion. That can be tough. No matter how much you enjoy the activity, a routine to rigidly stick to is challenging and proves that a habit also involves a precarious amount of effort, will power and motivation (of which we all don't constantly have because we aren't machines although society expects otherwise!).

Some people are more regimented than others, as I have noticed with my father who is German. His willpower inspires me because it never seemed like a battle for him to always be on task because it came at ease to him.

In general, the Germans truly are disciplined when it comes to working effort. Living here makes me aware of this. Yet again, everything is about balance. Seeing their strict routine of self-discipline in action showed me how anyone is capable of reigning and ruling their lifestyle if the right mindset is endorsed. If you yearn to better yourself every day then you are going to.

It also made me realise that I have a certain degree of discipline, but it also is hard for me on certain occasions when I simply am not down to do whatever I need to get done. Anyone can perform discipline, just as anyone can set targets, it is just the determination that triggers the ability for self-mastery to work. It cannot be birthed overnight, it takes time.

Be patient and see progress in something, always. Even the little things. Find progress and you will be presented with self-worth. If you are driven and determined that seeking out solitude will work magic within, then nothing can stop you. You see and feel the benefits, what better reason to keep going?! Growing towards self-awareness involves a pinch of persistence and a hand full of patience.

That is my opinion, but I see it evident in friends, clients and family members around me, as well as in myself. Open up your heart and create the art. Be it physical or mental. You are the only one that can start to put your energy in cultivating self-care in this aspect. Drive yourself to be determined, push yourself towards purpose - remember why. Become competent in devoting the time to the point where it will become a time of the day like dinner- crucial and critical to self-sustenance. You deserve it.

Centre yourself amid silence

Sitting with your feelings can be rough but courageous. Absence of sound leads to awareness of self. This is why escaping the noise and noticing silence is something special and we all need to do it to get back to our being. It takes time to truly get to know yourself in which you must spend time dealing with your emotions and thoughts all at once. It can feel overwhelming, to begin with, but as you let yourself settle and see things for what they are, the art of being on your own is healing and honourable in every sense.

It is a special kind of power when you can sit alone and deal with the daze that you are in as things arise and come as a surprise.

As far as I'm concerned, you should acknowledge how superior and strong you are when coming to reach into your mind because it is frightful, that is for sure. Now more than ever, mental health issues flooding the gates of children means we must take action.

Showing them how to take time out is absolutely imperative. The feeling of being alone is terrifying because it is in that moment that the monster of lies rushes in and tells you things that are absolutely shameful and sinful so that you cannot bear being on your own because hatred heightens. Being alone can shut you down or shoot you up in the sky, showering you with your craft of care.

The technique of managing your own company is straightforward: do something that you love, enjoy and entertain your creative spirit. Pick something that is not considered a chore that you might ignore. For some, cleaning is not a chore (like me hehe) because it is a mental shower. The tool kit to master solitude so that you feel complete on your own is to accept the given moment and feel rewarded that you have given yourself this moment to manifest your energy in. Restore, revive and feel alive. It is an achievement in itself.

We have thousands of distractions that make it more of an accomplishment to be able to switch off- literally. Switch off your phone. Switch off any other device that deters your mind to be in the present moment of purely focussing on you. It is a practice. Some may call this mindfulness. Bringing all your attention to the moment is something we are all capable of doing.

It takes time, as everything does. After all, it is a practice of self-care, so we should give our devoted attention. Take your focus away from anything that can be a distraction to delve deeper into your mind. Undivided attention to oneself initiates intuitiveness and welcomes self-worth, of which we can never fall short of.

Like anything in life that requires devotion and commitment, an array of other objectives come into play such as concentration and keenness. You must want to better yourself, to begin with, to thrive off solo time.

Create a sacred space for yourself, so that you know where to go when you seek out solitude. It could be the library, cafe or your room. Seek out space and drop down the pace.

This does not necessarily mean a physical location but somewhere you can be kind to yourself. It might mean a space in your mind that only you can access in a split second to get back to your breath and beyond. You could access this on a train and feel the rain of pain rush away.

It might involve a period in your day to see the sunrise and sunset seeping and shining its glory into your soul so that you can see the light of day with a fresh perspective. Give yourself permission to be silent and surrender to the moment and master the art of being free. When can you come to silence? A rare thing when you think about it, right? That is exactly why it is so special to see what magic you can make with the gift we can call silence.

Shower, bath, bake or cook - go with whatever warrants your full attention.

We suffer from noise-pollution so recognise silence as the solution.

To conclude...

Alone time feasts on lifting your state of mind so

that it can find peace and progress in a fashion to inhabit more frequently. One of the aims of seeking out solitariness is to pursue your ambitions and retreat from the inhibitions that are deterring you away from the power of peace within. When you come to be on your own and do things that you enjoy, things will feel right and realisation may set in about ways to make yourself happy without any added extras or conscious effort to be exalted.

We all find strength in solo time, it is just the time that is being neglected. New energy enters our lives daily, but it is up to us to decide how to deal with the blend so every situation endorses growth.

Entrust yourself with the job to take on new auras in ways that will only be beneficial so you can become more comfortable and courageous in the character you are building. You can either reach and receive something serviceable from the daily state of affairs by accepting everything for what it is or reject and reach back for comfort in procrastination. How can you serve yourself?

The easier option is to retract and retaliate against all the power that comes pounding in on you at once by fighting it off and frenzying in fear. If you give yourself the time to reflect on what is serving you and what is misleading you, then true acceptance will occur.

Negative vibes will always make their way through, but it is how you handle them that engages with inner freedom. This openness will show you are capable of anything if you believe in it. A state of mind that engages with bad auras will be brought down easily, whereas if you don't choose to be beaten by outside elements then may you be closer to achieving peace.

If you constantly complain, then negative energy will build shackles, whereas if you comply and endure negative energy as lessons and life, then the restraints will be released.

If empowerment is employed through self-care and self-love then solitude will grant you gladness, influencing every experience to be a new and niche opportunity to mould and make the way you like to light up your life.

Use every lesson as a tool to become more self-sufficient.

Learn to love yourself

Everyone advises it, but what does it mean? How do we conquer it, and why do we need to?

For starters, I am not here to preach but to guide. Throughout the whole book, that has been my intention. You can listen or you can ignore, either way you are the one that decides to do something or nothing. Learn from it or lump it! It is up to you to discover your love within; waiting to be lit up like a fuzzy fine fire erupting with peace, acceptance and strength if treated with care, consideration and contentment. The abundance of actions concerned with loving yourself takes a lot of courage and care; including relentless showers of forgiveness.

It is sad to say we are stuck in finding meaning in other places rather than the place that is a priority in reaching loving oneself; self-awareness. It begins with you and ends with you (literally u hehe). So how do you love yourself? Well, I'm not here to tell you to do this, do that. I am here to tell you what I do, so you may observe what is right for you. Neither can I tell you how - it is up to you to explore. I am here to guide and encourage you to find techniques and methods to make all your dreams come true. The answer lies within you.

We are only complete until we learn to love ourselves wholly. However, we live in a world that strives to put us off the true tracks in defining our importance and knowing we are enough. You are enough. That is what we are never told through campaigns, adverts and marketing, otherwise, they would not get our money. Nevertheless, money does not hold the key to happiness nor to loving yourself. Just wanted to make that clear right from the start...!

Loving yourself involves an array of affairs with acceptance, awareness, and appreciation at the centre. When performed with practicality, it doesn't have to be difficult. Accepting your physical self comes from mental belief. Mental and physical work together for the best here. Self-love can provide contentment, streaming through like a rushing river.

Here are some ways to shift self-loathing for self-loving:

- Nurturing your thoughts with care and consideration. Taking control of them - that is the only thing you want to control here.

- Master your thoughts the same way you control what you wear, what you eat.

- Become proud of who you are, no matter where you are at in life. Willingly look in the mirror daily and smile, noticing your imperfections and rejoicing in them.

- Saying no when it gets too much or saying yes when you want to progress.

- Feeling comfortable in your skin, so that positive vibes pour out your pores.

- Dismiss other people's perceptions because the inner peace you have reached is more than enough.

- Emanate the love with others as a by-product of the love you have stored within, shining like a star.

How?

So clearly the list of self-love is endless. It all depends on you. It can involve a to-do list (I know we love them these days and I am all for them!) They work well with self-love because loving yourself is unique and individual to every one of our needs. Loving you is suited to you, nobody else. Being OK with who is birthed from within, digging deep in the realms of right now and realising your potential.

Loving yourself is based on a foundation of self-esteem. That is, not the ego; something sinister and sewn to unloving deeds. It can be hard to build your base with love considering the cracks in our foundation from life's trials and tribulations taunt us to continuously question our worth. Am I enough? Do I deserve love? Why does nobody love me? Do not worry.

Loving yourself is intentional. No matter how tortured or torn down your foundation is, there is always a chance to restock your solid foundation of bricks back up again, one by one. Show yourself the attention, awareness and acceptance that you deserve and take baby steps.

Imagine yourself as a flower:

They require water. They require light. Then what? They look pretty and they grow. You are exactly the same: you must be watered with kindness and grace. When you shower yourself with self-love, you will come to love yourself better than anyone else ever could or can.

That is the aim of self-love. It is in your hands only. Investing in yourself is the best thing you can do to reach your potential, gain clarity and the ability to accept yourself for all your flaws, fantasies and findings. Be intuitive. Take the initiative. Be intentional. You do you, then the rest will follow like a dog obediently scurrying along after its owner because loving yourself attracts others. You will share the love because of the love resounding within.

Love is infectious. When you honour yourself, others will be attracted to you. When you accept yourself, others have no choice but to. Why? Because you are the law of attraction. It makes sense to concentrate on healing within so you will shimmer and sparkle outwardly. It is called investment into your being, essentially the most important and sacred thing we all have the honour to do, so let us learn how.

We all know how to do it, so why aren't we? Simple. The world messes with our love to make us feel like we are not in control, but they are. Who are they? The media, politicians, food chains, shops etc etc. We are taught to love others, but where does the love come from? Our society spurs us on to believe that we should seek love from the outside and then we will feel complete. Our culture redefines our idea of self-love, clouding our view of beauty. Our Beauty is based on perspective within society, whereas our true beauty is breathed in our souls.

If you change your view to see the beauty in everything, you may just learn how to love yourself inside out. There is something for you to love everything and everyone. Find these things. Make it your daily duty. Unravel what you love about others and learn to love it about yourself. It could be that you're body-conscious. Firstly, we all are at some point in our life.

Here's my body-conscious story: I remember when I was a teenager and I wanted bigger boobs (didn't we all!), but I only started to love my iron chest (nickname on behalf of my mum!) when I realised that this is what I have got and I might as well make the most of it.

You see, if you are comfortable with yourself, then others will be too. Ok, so you still want a breast enlargement? Why? Will it make you feel better because others will look at you or will it make you feel better because you will like what you see in the mirror? Think of the real reason. Dig deep. Ok, so you still want it because it will allow you to accept yourself. Why? We are all different and unique in our shapes and sizes.

It is awesome! Once I noticed this fact, I played on it. I praised my flat bum and flat chest and noticed other things I liked about myself. There's no need to concentrate on one part of your body you don't feel comfortable with because then you will lose sight of everything else that is beautiful about you. I have a hairy face, meaning I have a moustache. Greek-inspired from my Greek mother.

I remember as a child my sister (ten years my age) would dye her moustache regularly. It marvelled me. Moreso because my mum tended to point mine out too. I got taunted for it at school, as you do. "Why have you got a moustache?" I tell you what, being asked at that time as a puberty potent teen was horrifying. I hid my upper lips all the time, either with my hand or the magic Rimmel cover stick. It didn't work much. There came a point in my life where I looked in the mirror and thought - who cares? I'm not going to go to the extent of shaving it off or dying it.

(That would just add effort into my daily routine!)

Realising that if I don't care, then somebody else's opinion didn't mean much. Don't get me wrong, the bullying still took its toll, but we all have been there.

They do it because they are either:
1) Jealous (hard to believe they would envy my facial hair, but yeah)
2) Hate themselves
3) Don't have anything better to do
4) Want to feel superior over you, and bring you down

    I realised bullies bring brash comments to light because they think others will get a laugh out of it too. Laugh with them. Why not? The more laid back about it you seem to be, the less they will want to pick on you. Don't let it get to you. Go with it.

    Think of it this way- what someone finds repulsive about you, another person might find fascinating. Now I went with a technique that could help you, too...

    I found features on my face I loved instead, like my eyes. I loved putting mascara and eyeliner on, drawing attention to my upper face rather than bottom part (although my cheeks are masked with hairs too). Finding acceptance in your imperfections is the best way. What you might find ugly, someone might find pretty. It was only when a guy I was dating told me he liked my hairy face that I couldn't stop laughing. Howling with disbelief, I asked, "WHY!?". "It's cute", he replied. It was at that moment I realised it doesn't matter what anybody thinks, as long as I learn to love myself for who I am, then comfort can shed through. Learn to laugh at yourself, giggle at others when they try to tease you. Laughing beats everything. Deal with your imperfections, or rather be proud of them because nobody is going to do it for you. Every minor detail makes you... YOU. Remember that.

It is not someone's job to like you - it is yours.

Ok, so for some, the prospect of loving may be quite daunting or humiliating because being ashamed of oneself occurs commonly in our corrupt world. It could be considered as an imperative implanted on us by our self-centred system of the West. For others, it may be shrugged off to not be taken seriously because it is only for those spiritual folk or religious individuals that can attain such a love. Seriously, I've gotten that before- ah you're just a hippie or a god freak. Whatever the term, people throw it around heartlessly because they have still yet to find their magic. The magic is in you, so let us grasp this potential that is ready to be awakened inside of every one of us.

The love within will take you far. Nobody will be your why because you will have wings to fly sky high.

Get to know yourself

Loving yourself entails a healthier and happier you, where it is crucial to care for your well-being. Turning up the temperature of self-love lets others heat up towards your energy. It's like a pot of curry, infusing in all its spices for a while. When you come to taste it, the texture, smell and flavour take over. Your pot of self-love is the same: learn to let it stew, so others can take from it too.

People will be able to connect with you on a deeper level as acceptance and awareness rise from your commitment.

If you love yourself you are putting yourself as the leader of your fulfilment which is vital for finding love, peace and joy in everyday life. You are the first one and the last one that loves you, so make it worthwhile!

Think about it- we are with ourselves more than anyone. I only really noticed this recently. I've been spending a lot of time looking for jobs or feeling, well, overwhelmed. I have to deal with myself, my thoughts, my habits. One way or another if I have to be with myself forever, I might as well make it fun.

Dance with the possibility of endlessly loving yourself. Laugh, love and learn with your constant development.

But I get it, who are you? Why are you here? Such questions creep up when we are isolated and lonely, feeling like failures. Loving ourselves seems far in the distance. Be fragile with yourself. Treat yourself like a child.

Every single person ponders about who they are at some point in their life. It is frightening to be in a position where you feel further away from yourself than ever before, but it is also normal. Sometimes we are disconnected. Why? Well, what did you check before? Your phone, your laptop, some sort of technological device is definitely in your vicinity. Our world right now is so connected that it has resulted in us being disconnected to ourselves more than ever.

Loneliness is an epidemic on a world-scale and it is manifesting its harm within children now too. Just a drastic statistic to back this up (gets me every time): according to a study by Action for Children, 1 in 3 children suffer from symptoms of loneliness (and this was back in 2017).

https://www.cypnow.co.uk/news/article/one-in-three-children-suffer-from-loneliness

So yes, this is real. Now let's try to deal:

It is OK to not know who you are, it is not OK for other people to tell you who you are.

It is OK to not feel OK, it is not OK to feel guilty.

It is OK to not know where you are going, it is not OK to think everybody has their shit together and you are the only one with no plan.

It is OK to not know what to do, it is not OK for other people to tell you what to do.

It is up to you to know your passions and pick what is best for you. Something so sane sounding should be one of the first things we are taught because it may be the toughest to accomplish and achieve throughout life.

Well, think about it: from a young age, we are taught to love ourselves in little steps- tying our laces, taking our first steps, riding our first bike. All these occasions involve internal acceptance and courage. On top of that, we are praised for them all. So what should we be doing more of? Praising! Never stop praising yourself! Humbly write down three things every day that you are proud of achieving. They can be so simple like making a good dinner or doing the washing. Something that has worked its magic on your self-love. For waking up, eating, doing your thang - praise yourself for the little things. Never stop doing it.

Being yourself means to be ready, be complete, be assertive, be free, be grateful, be alive.

For the sake of how much I love the value of writing lists (otherwise I wouldn't get anything done!) let us imagine that loving yourself involves a multitude of actions, multiplied daily based upon our individual needs. Let us not be swayed by a list and desire to vigorously pursue each point to achieve the goal, however, make it a goal every day. Yes, you read that right.

Every single day. Make it your goal to love yourself, first thing in the morning. I normally wake up and do the whole shebang straight away. Pee, brush my teeth, wash my face, feel fresh. When doing that, putting on a cup of tea is bliss. I feel like I have already started to serve myself in liking who I am.

Ok, it's not like that every day - some days can be laidback (not necessarily a fail) and you can't get up. In this case, try your best to do tiny things and they will mount up to be big things. Write down your feelings and notice why, how you feel this way. Take care of yourself and love will reward you. Sounds simple? Is simple. Step by step.

It is a sound start to simply write down what you love about yourself and hate about yourself, to begin with. Do not worry about writing so many points, nor should you fret if the negative outweighs the positive. Just write what you feel, and the rest will follow.

What is with all this list writing? I get it- currently, we can't get enough of it. Well, writing lists allows us to reflect. Reflection is one of the key ingredients in the concoction of coming to love yourself and can sometimes be regarded as criticism. Write down and rise above. Installing involvement in something bigger is why lists are so attractive to do.

We are all hard on ourselves, no matter who we are, where we are from, nor how successful or rich/poor we are. It comes in waves of anxiety or flashes of ecstasy. Fault-finding comes naturally to us as humans, but we must be ready to criticise ourselves as well as praise ourselves. Positive and negative come hand in hand.

Without positive attributes, you will not have negative notions. We are wired to worry and be weary, yet we are also in charge of rewiring our mind by managing our thoughts and determining our actions. It is how you overcome the condemnation by challenging its worth of existence. This is the essence of overcoming criticism with care and consideration. When writing the list, it might have been easier for the hateful and harmful ideas to arise rather than aspects that you appreciate about yourself. It is OK.

This is also something that must be learnt on the route to self-love: turn doubt into appreciation and criticism into praise.

Who said you aren't good enough? NOBODY.

Am I good enough? This type of personal interrogation slithers its way to infect us all at some point in our lives. It is similar to a virus, infecting us all at some point or other in life, awaiting its entrance at any point ready to prance on our peace aspired to attain during daily life. The probing lingers in our appearance and manifests itself in our beautiful minds, which then turns into destructive thoughts and depressing emotions clambering to cling on to any crumb of consideration for ourselves.

Criticism cannot be effective unless you acknowledge it in a way that will allow you to learn and grow from. One may identify this as "constructive criticism": confessing to the critique and fighting it off with a fruitful condition based upon bettering yourself and the situation.

So, when you feel like you are not good enough, do not beat yourself up about it by boarding the roller-coaster of rejection, instead acknowledge the cruel critique and recognise where it has catalysed from. Awareness is the answer. Acceptance is the antidote. "Being good enough" can only gage trauma and tantrum if you support it to act on your emotions. Believe in its power and you will give it the right to live. It is like a headache - it is harder to get rid of when you think about it and don't do anything about it. When you get a cup of tea or some oil, the symptoms can go sooner rather than later.

You are the master of self-love, nobody else. When we feel down, we tend to fully emerge ourselves into performing self-pity and thus end up easily wallowing in our pot of home-made misery. The more we stir up the commotion of our self-doubt with a spoon full of sadness and a pinch of pity, the harder it is to separate the ingredients and conquer what is wrong with us in the first place, getting lost in the product rather than recognising the recipe. Ingredients are key, go over it. Take things out that don't tickle your taste buds and disgust you.

When we do not believe in ourselves to be good enough for any predicament, person or place then we end up comparing ourselves to others. Comparing yourself to others and feeling worthless is also natural, but it also takes on the form of fanaticism as we soon forget that we are all individual human beings, of whom none are perfect in any way, shape or form. If none of us is perfect, then there is no reason to not feel good enough. Aim to feel good because good enough does not exist. You are more than good enough, believe it, be it, live it.

Unfortunately, such a staggering thought can be probed by other people. Guess what?! They are not worth it either-- simple as. If someone does not deem you good enough, then they are far from being at peace with themselves, compelled to inflict someone else with the burden because they wish to bring someone else down to their miserable level.

At other times it is because they believe they want the best for you, so pushing you to be a better person allows them to believe that they are helping you out in a flimsy fashion. This is, however, not the case. Nobody enjoys nor appreciates being told that they are not good enough. And as a product of this to be told what to do...

Think about it for a moment. It is essentially impossible to measure what this concept of being 'good enough' itself even means.

No chart, list or graph can guide us in being the worldly sought concept of being good enough. I have moments of mashed up mental madness, where I think I am not good enough for a job or my partner. I have to pinch myself and bring myself back to reality when this happens. It happens to all of us. That devil in our brain is a battle to quieten. One way I like to dismiss the good enough whisper is to write down how I feel. Journal, jot down and drive away from the bad spirit.

Good enough standard set out by religion:

All in all, everyone experiences their happiness carefully crafted by themselves. Yes, there are commandments, rules and regulations that people follow to be a good person. For example, in every religion, a basis is laid out defined by moral deeds that exhibit love and prohibit hatred. Christianity speaks of treating others as you would like to be treated and many other mandatory missions that make you a good person.

Good enough set out by society:

I believe this "good enough" term has descended from society, capitalism and consumerism. We compare, we want more, we look up to idols and others in not only one way. Turn it around. Make it about you.

Good enough is based on you and how you are reaching your full potential. Being good is based on your morals, thoughts and actions. Consider this next time you don't feel good enough...

It is up to us to strive to be a good person but never mislead our fragile mind to engage in dishonouring our beautiful being by thinking, hearing or considering that we are never good enough. Once you believe in yourself then this will not matter. Your magic matters the most.

Good enough for what? We are all good enough to be blessed with a life, so live it and love it. We all came out of our mum's vagina and have daily poops (sorry for the grotesque facts, just trying to make a point). There is a serious danger in denying yourself of your power, so protect it. The prime indicator to love yourself is to pursue positive acts of goodness so the power of happiness and provoke self-acceptance. Forget about being good enough and focus on being good.

^ work on this last part!

Defeat the self-pity and crown yourself with confidence:

Be it an infliction of self-doubt provoked personally

or evoked by other people, you can overcome it. The power is within. Train your mind to acknowledge, but not react. Train your mind to reflect, but not neglect. Let's say negative connotations from others controls how you feel and act, so you decide to drown in self-pity because there is no other way out. Hold up, there is! The image you have of yourself overtakes anybody's opinions of you. That is called confidence. It is in reach for anyone, with a handful of belief, a pinch of banter and a spoon of sensitivity.

The opinion of yourself matters most. This self-belief can defeat self-pity and is already a step closer in being a better person.

Question: how does it make you feel when someone denies your strength? Shit, right? How does it feel when you are sure of yourself? Amazing, right? (Maybe you're not there yet, but it doesn't matter you will...)

Welcome your inner strength, planted within each one of us by affirming your love every damn day. Make it a duty, a habit. It is your responsibility to awaken your potential, nobody else's. Awaken it through accepting yourself fully: not only your physical looks but what lies within. Your intentions, your kindness, your compassion, your reason to wake up in the morning. Finding meaning manifests respect and the right to be yourself. Your strength is readily available to arouse and utilise at any given point.

Finding the strength is the trickiest task at hand, but we are all made of it (sparking in dire situations when strength is the only answer). For example, we are made of resilience. Take a testing time of your life- you can just sit back and not go anywhere, but most of the time you have to push through... that is life.

When the worst phone call of my life hit me out of the blew, I was blasted with utter misery. I was watching Sherlock Holmes with my mum after having my wisdom teeth taken out (physical pain was being soothed by Ben and Jerry's) when my best friend's step mum rang me. He was dead. I couldn't believe it - just like that, he was gone and there was nothing I could do. Nothing was in my power anymore to help him (I had been helping him through anxiety, depression and drug-problem-polluted days for the past four years at this point). My power was to help myself overcome it and learn from it. My task was clear: I had to forgive myself and be strong. I had no other choice but to be brave. Self-love was my medicine.

You must utilise this strength to stretch your limitations. If you are ready to take on critique in every shape or form, then you will learn from every lesson on your doorstep, digging deeper in self-love. Strength comes at times of grief, loss and heartbreak. Strength is a powerful force that keeps us going, resilience becomes your reason to keep going. Resilience comes from developing a positive frame of mind and it is in your reach to find. Although this sounds effortless, when you know how to evoke strength from just one certain situation then you will have truly discovered how to access and engage your inner strength to defeat unhappiness.

I truly believe that the strength of loving yourself is

immeasurable and cannot be blown down when secured. Once I realised that I am in control of my happiness, I was able to access it at any time I wanted by appreciating, forgiving, accepting, participating in acts of gratitude (yet again the list goes on!) and it is all about working on yourself as a by-product of loving yourself.

There was a point when I did not love myself. I searched for love and thought that every one of us looked for love to feel complete. I am fortunate enough to have been shown love in such wondrous ways by my amazing support system of friends and family, so I took that, cherished it and learnt from it. Even when you are loved from a young age, it doesn't mean you know how to love yourself. There is no 5-step guide we are given as children, it is up to us to discover techniques in achieving it. You must love yourself first to accept the love from others and it is only when we get older that we may realise this.

In my teens, I always wanted people to like me (especially boys) and I still felt incomplete. You can never be "completed" by another person because you first have to find completion through your self-acceptance. I wished to love myself, so I started to do things for myself such as praying, doing yoga, reading, writing. I then realised we look for love to be understood because it is the most powerful and precious thing we all have the honour in harvesting.

Criticism is like a cloud - it moves quickly and joins others to form a storm of torment and terror. It rains on your parade. It piles up like a list of to-dos. However, the storm can be stopped by showering yourself with consideration rather than criticism. Yes, you gathered correctly- the sun is a vision of acceptance here, clearing the clouds for new rays of positivity to shine through. There is no need to feel offended, ashamed or tortured by someone's judgment. Listen and don't let it get to you. Feel anger or torment, like any other emotion, but do not attach yourself. Envision all your emotions like clouds, coming and going.

Exceeding in self-love is the remedy of realisation.

When you love yourself so much and are truly happy in your skin, criticism cannot catch fire to the soul as the ego is equalled out. Taking your ego away so it is not on display will broaden your perspective to see the world in a better way. Managing this part can be pragmatic rather than idealistic. It all starts with how you combat judgment, remarks and fear. Criticise yourself constructively, learn from your love and understanding rather than put yourself down with harsh dismissal. Do not be afraid to admit to what is wrong so that you are not overwhelmed with worry.

You are only human and sometimes the world expects us to prove our worth. You don't need to. If you love yourself, there is no need to prove yourself to anyone. Let go and love inward. Observe but don't preserve. Turn critique into a challenge and prove yourself to you - that is what is most important.

If you hold on to the thought of not being good enough or any other belittling bewilderment, you will only trap yourself into a cage of insecurity shackled with chains of self-image, self-respect, self-worth etc.

(this list, unfortunately, does go on!) As we sometimes step into the cage without realising the consequences, it can be harder to escape from all the fetters of self-remorse as they mentally and physically lock you in.

Come to realise that you are associating yourself to words of utter nonsense. They are words, they come and they go. Words are nothing. Words are everything. You are something. Everything you need is within you. All these negative connotations, at the end of the day, are only words that do not mean a thing.

If you relate yourself to dispiriting language then you will keep falling into the never-ending pit of misery. If you revive yourself with uplifting words then you will keep encouraging wisdom into your life.

It is commendable not to listen to the inner-demon that wishes you to spiral downwards, whispering sour nothings into your ear. Do not affix yourself to any of it. Sing a song, read a poem, ring your friend. Find ways that will off-put the negative chatter.

Attachment is fatal. As soon as you connect yourself with a statement or figure of speech, you allow your mind to further fantasize on the idea, envisaging yourself as it is. You become the word because you let it. You are the one that visualizes, believes, imagines...

You are the one that lets it live or you are the one that lets it go. Combat it with a positive thought, defend it with a smile, and hit it with a strike of self-love and appreciation so that it cannot last or linger longer than you can ponder on the feeling. Distract yourself to be free of insecurity and uncertainty by distancing yourself from the pressures that surround you and embrace the person that you are. It is a process to remember, only practice makes perfect. Acknowledge, distract and detach. Seek out your method to realise your powerful potential. Be free.

There is a method used to remember things by associating an image to release absent-mindedness actions. For example, if you look into the fridge and forget what you are going in there for (everyone does it!), then you imagine cows coming out at you (for the milk of course!). Attaching an image with an object allows for your memory to not get the better of you. The same may be applied when a discouraging word or thought pops into your mind. Let's say it is "I don't believe in myself", with the keyword being the belief, or rather disbelief.

Whenever anything concerning disbelief appears into your mind associate it with a dragon. The dragon suddenly opens its mouth and fire comes out dismantling any reason for disbelief to exist in your frame of mind. The dragon is your guardian angel when it comes to disbelief, always on watch and will fend for your right of self-belief. Use any animal, natural element, plant, whatever suits your fancy!

Nobody can believe in yourself more than you.

Believe in Yourself.

Loving yourself is not something to be achieved or accomplished in accordance with a specific list of "do this" or "don't do that". It is tailored to your individual needs, linked to your likes and induced by your interests. It is your personal to-do list. I am sick of seeing all these lists splashed over social media (although I know they are only for good intentions!), but your list will only let you go further.

You are the one that can find out what it is that makes you tick and makes you break, so that you may manage your mind to live a life full of peace, joy and love. Someone, like a coach or therapist, may be your guide in this by asking you questions and putting things into perspective, but you are the one that has to mind map and make decisions. You can be your own worst enemy or your own best friend- you choose. Choose the one that will motivate you to employ emotions that lift you up instead of drag you down. Remember: you are love. One cannot conquer a list of self-love actions, otherwise, we would all be called human borings not human beings. Life is a journey of self-discovery, where some fully seclude themselves from worldly evils to experience what some may view as the highest tranquillity, as the monks do.

Whereas, others wish to be heavily involved with healing humanity by helping others out. We are all different in discovering our own true happiness, but if you truly wish to be happy then the realisation of caring and loving for yourself yields many benefits to thrive in leading a jovial journey of life. Just be wary to not isolate yourself from your full potential, of which you can only unlock. People may assist in pushing you there, but you are the one that gets there.

A predominant part of loving yourself concerns believing in yourself, so you will be the authentic individual knighted in all your splendour and glory. This then allows you to radiate peace, love and joy to all those around you. We must love ourselves to feel fine in our own skin and lead a happy life. But getting there is the difficult part that many struggle with their whole lives. This should not be the case. We, instead, concentrate on cumbersome antics and worry about tomorrow, in turn damaging our soul and deterring us away from our light within. One of my favourite scriptures in the bible that I refer to in times of worry is: "Therefore do not worry about tomorrow, for tomorrow will worry about itself. Each day has enough trouble of its own." (Matthew 6:34) How about take your favourite uplifting quote, scripture or mantra and allow it to comfort you when you feel far away from yourself. Let it bring you back. Hang it up. Take each day as it is. Accept every day as a new day to accept yourself. When you start to believe in a quote and apply it to your being, then will self-love light up your life.

Tip: I love to plaster my bathroom mirror above the sink with yogitea quotes (it was seen as my mark in University when all my flatmates knew they were there because of me!). I like to centre my attention on one when brushing my teeth in the morning and repeat it to myself. When looking in the mirror and doing this, the floodgates of fruitfulness unbolt as you are opening up to the boundless hope that is stored within. Believe in yourself every morning... your true self is waiting somewhere deep within to be exposed and embraced so you can be what you want to be.

Accept yourself for who you are

Unfortunately, the tricks and trade of the world do not support us to be ourselves, so it is not as simple as it should be. If it were easy, our consumerist society would not succeed to the extent that it does. The advertising industry serves the fact that we feel insecure in ourselves, feeding off of our self-esteem issues rather than focusing on what feels good to nurture our needs. Dependency on materialistic items does not let you love yourself as the raw and radiant character that you are. Dependency on celebrities cannot incline you to be yourself, but a modified version dependent on them, nor can many more artificial addictions and harmful habits that this world misleads us to deem crucial to true fulfilment. We must be the person we aspire to be, otherwise, we will torture ourselves from inside out: this is exactly what is happening...

Our world is wired to charge itself from our insecurities, lack of faith and anxiety so that retail can raid not only our closets but our inner storeroom full of doubt, distrust and disbelief raring to be restored. We do not feel complete, so we look outside for the answer. Think about it. The marketing of retail therapy to lavish lifestyles guide us in thinking that happiness is accessible through seeking out man-made richness. Sorry to say, but the more you seek out those riches created by the human race, the less love you will feel for yourself as you become dependent on external factors that forbid us to flourish and bloom. Striving for satisfaction must come from within and begin with treating yourself right. May it be taking a long bath or cold shower, having a laughing fit with friends, exercising, gardening, practising meditation, listening to music, going on a long walk, reading a book (you get the gist!). The list goes on… yet it takes effort. An effort that requires you to take care of your well-being and peace of mind. When you invest time in the things that make you feel good, then you will participate in accepting who you are and loving yourself.

Write down what you love to do for yourself, it can be as simple as cooking or chilling with friends. Let the list be tips to love yourself. A pick me up.

Whenever you don't feel yourself, pick it up, take a peek and practice the fine art of self-love. You are your own artist when it comes to loving yourself, so get your groove on with getting to know how you can fully flourish like that flower we envisioned, to begin with.

Take your time

To love yourself, you must focus your attention inwards. Find what feels good. All these activities announce your ability to love yourself, truly and kindly where effort in taking time out with yourself is fundamental in the equation. Notice something special: these past-times do not require spending money but spending the most precious thing we all have on this world – time. Time is precious. Time is of the essence. Take time out from always trying to live up to the standards set out by others and expectations… just stay still. When you are still with yourself, you may feel funny and fanatic to some degree as emotions and thoughts flood the mind and overtake your body. Allow it to be. Admit yourself to acknowledge each emotion that you feel float by so that you can get to know yourself in every way possible. Practising this will allow you to accept each emotion as it comes and goes, recognising that everything is fleeting. As the adage reminds us "this too shall pass", we come to realise that be it happiness or sadness; everything is temporary. Feel everything, don't feel bad for anything. It is only human.

You are in control of how long you feel an emotion, so you can be in control of who you are or want to be. This practice can be identified as meditation or simply coming to silence with the self and soul. For the sake of labelling everything nowadays, let us just take a moment to ponder on how such a self-help method can only bring positivity and self-love into your life.

It is irrefutable that meditation enables you to find yourself due to the silent sentience of your own being. It has been proven that the effects of meditation make a positive mark on your mind. Like everything, it takes time (but not that long!). It is a journey of letting go of every thought to accept yourself for who you are in the present moment. By doing this, you will extract your consciousness and attract confidence. We all have it within us, it is just the time and effort that people struggle with these days to grant themselves the time of day to feel the flow of letting go. Start with 5 minutes a day and go from there.

Take time out with people you love

We unintentionally abuse ourselves a lot of the time, adhering to the ways of our society by depending on short-term fulfilment set out to us like the standard norm. Go against it. But I get it; sometimes a soup of self-help advice does not switch on your light, and it is easier to scroll through some friends' photos that produce erratic emotions of jealousy and envy.

That is the way it is. How you feel is much deeper and darker entering the realms of your soul when you are alone, so you escape that obscurity by seeking out short-lived gratification. These fluctuating feelings of happiness cannot count towards self-fulfilment though, instead, they chip away at the soul.

When you realise everything is transitory and you are the one rising, that is the moment you can truly learn to love yourself. How? Through smiling, laughing and interacting with people you love. These genuine moments might be when you can be your best self (and will be when you are your worst self too!). Utilise them to see yourself for who you are. Who do you want to be, how do you want to better yourself etc.

Enable these times to enhance your being and bring out the best in your character. Ok, so sometimes spending time with loved ones will shape you into someone you aren't normally around others and that is totally normal. We are our raw, mad and maze-like selves surrounded by the people we are closest to because there is no filter. We are who we are. It can be good and bad at the same time, don't beat yourself up about it- learn from it.

Spending time with your family and friends will enable you to see yourself with no added extras. It will open your mind to the real you, as you commit acts of care and consideration as well as sporadic sessions of shouting as siblings or family members seem to test your patience. It is clear to say that you can learn a lot about yourself in these instants of instantaneous actions, thoughts and words that seep from your untethered soul.

These are the uncensored moments full of passion and pronounce you to be you. Encounter mishap, embrace frustration, confront kindness and conclude with love. From there on, you may engage with yourself and see why the people who love you the most actually love you for who you are (and hate you!).

Fall in love with yourself

Learning to love yourself consists of falling in love with yourself. It's a "says it on the lid" kind of thing. So, if you are searching for that one person to love you: look in the mirror. It starts with you and ends with you. If there is one thing you have taken away from this book I hope it is the manner in how to love yourself.

Remember this: there is only one you and that should be enough reason to be you with all your defects and delights that make you, you. You are entitled to be you, even as the fear feeds on your soul to seek out to be like someone else at times.

It happens. Doubts arise, fears coincide. Who are you? I am not talking about personality, I am talking about the pure, uncensored version of yourself that you only allow out at night just before you go to bed when brushing your teeth as you glance in the mirror and pull funny faces.

When you snuggle your hand under your pillow looking out at the blackness before drifting off with all the thoughts stirring around your mind... or when you just wake up in the morning, untouched face and unbrushed teeth in your natural state seemingly ready and reborn (or not!) to take on a new day. Strip yourself of your hair, eyes and physical features. That is not you.

Of course, it is true that one must feel comfortable in their own skin to fully love themselves, but what is most important is loving yourself for all your flaws to fully fall in love with one's essence.

This is exactly what we do when we fall in love- we love the other person for who they are, accepting their flaws and failures, yet recognising them to be the person they are. You become enthralled by every aspect of them (and annoyed at others!), but you would not change them for the world (at first!), deepening your attraction to them. So why don't we fall in love with ourselves in the exact same way?

It is not just a choice to become captivated by ourselves, but an honour that we must not deny ourselves from discovering our own brilliant nature and bright light day by day.

It's quite curious we all yearn to feel loved and crave falling in love when we have the privilege to love ourselves first. Act on it. Only then can we share that love with someone else. It is totally natural to need love and crave the deep desirable type of admiration that only one special person can show us; we are only human. Conversely, sometimes we depend so much on this kind of love out of fear, steering us to despair and discouragement in our hearts that we feel can only be filled by our other half.

We should not be scared when it comes to loving ourselves, as we have been made to do so. It is our responsibility, our gift. There is an unconditional love ready to be uprooted within every one of us. Find ways to captivate yourself by your ethereal being, be enthralled. Appreciate yourself for the little things: how you smile, how you frown, how you look down when you get shy or all-around when embarrassed. You are your own gardener when it comes to empowering and enriching the love that is stored within you to bloom and grow. Water yourself with compliments before anybody else can. Then, when you receive a compliment it will be more flattering with the knowledge that you accept the remark to be real.

There is nothing more attractive than being confident in yourself. I promise you. And so you should be. Audrey Hepburn indicated that "Beauty is being the best possible version of yourself, inside and out." If you are sure of yourself, there is no reason for anybody else to doubt you and the energy that you extract and attract. When you love yourself, you will not be hindered by anyone's thoughts or displeased by somebody's opinion. Be so sure of yourself that nobody can put you down. They will still try, but you are in control of how it makes you feel. Shrug it off. Ah well, whatever. You are more than that.

Yet again, remember that this is not about being attractive and alluring the one true love in, but it is about firstly finding yourself then letting everything else follow through. You are your first love. Falling in love with yourself is the moment you realise that perfection is found in all your imperfections. Feeling complete as the person you are is essential in any functioning and flourishing relationship. It does not concern selfishness but concentrates on selflessness. You must love yourself to have a healthy and happy relationship, able to accept love from somebody else because you can recognise every quality that they appreciate in you. This is when they will truly be able to bring out the best in you because you are accepting of the love you deserve.

Acknowledge yourself, accept yourself and assert yourself. When you feel good about yourself in ways only you can access, there is no denying that you will love yourself for who you are. Let us step back for a second and take an example. An aspect about yourself can be physical, but the quality is something so much more than what lies on the outside as it grows from within and shines to the outer world. Your voice. It is known to be that people don't like the sound of their own voices, so why would we love this part of ourselves?

I am not talking about your actual voice, I am talking about the way you pronounce certain words and hesitate before stringing them all together or have a higher pitch when you get excited about something and go lower when you are uncertain. Each and every one of us sound different and speak in our own special way. When you realise the tone or pace that you speak, you will come to realise what kind of person you are. I am no expert in this field of voices, so to say, but I do believe that you can learn a lot about a person by the way they speak. So, let yourself learn from it, the same goes to a lot of other motions and actions that you utter on a daily basis. It's like self-meditation.

Indulge in supporting each and every action you do so that you can feel a peace spark from within that is ready to love, encourage and be kind. If you are able to ignite this fire, then what is to follow will be pure happiness and acceptance. Loving yourself might be a tricky and tense path, to begin with, but like any adventure, once you have started you will not want to stop. There will be rocky roads on the way as any other relationship, but each stone is a lesson to learn from, grow and get better at being you. Whenever you give yourself time, your mind and body will react positively, so there is nothing to be frightened about.

Remove the fear from discovering who you are and permit yourself to ponder, reflect and realise who you want to be in order to love yourself to the best of your ability. Love yourself then the gates of acceptance will open up to the love affair that life has to offer.

Accept and appreciate yourself for who you are, you will get far. Once you realise that you are worthy of the love you deserve, self-love will become a daily antique actively anticipated to better yourself. The more you love yourself, the less you seek validation. The more you love yourself, the less you search for fulfilment.

The more you love yourself, the more energy is attracted to you. The more you love yourself, the more powerful you become in being an attractive source of happiness, stability and independence to make a positive change on Earth. Why? Because love puts you in harmony with the universe. You can be who you want to be, all it takes is love, peace and healing.

Falling in love begins with why and ends with you.

But sometimes it's not that easy, I feel you. When falling into a depression and having signs of schizophrenia, I didn't know what to do, but I knew I had to do something to get out of it. Opening up to friends was a starter.

THE MAIN course was coming to terms with my illness and the dessert was giving myself the time to actually get through it.

What's your starter, main, dessert?

Write it out and see how you feel. Remember that every day is a new day to take one step at a time. For me at one point, that even meant waking up and brushing my teeth. Even showering. When you get to the bathroom, look in the mirror and do this:

A little but lovely love yourself morning and evening practice:

1) Put your hand on your heart (this releases oxytocin)

2) Look at yourself in the mirror

3) Now say 'I love you'

4) Feel the kindness and compassion seep through your heart as you feel the beat and the buzz of the energy reveal itself to you at its purest state – you **are** love.

Acknowledgements

Although I didn't write this book during my psychotic episode in the mental clinic, I decided to publish it during that time of January, and it helped lift me out of the deep darkness I was going through. Some people were by my side every step of the way that I must acknowledge in the remaking of my optimistic self (of whom I never thought would return at one point).

First, I want to thank my parents for being by my side. My family would do anything for me, and I am so thankful for them. Without my dad physically being next to me during my mental clinic stay, I would've been lost. He brought me light when I was in darkness and hope when I felt numb. You were my angel from God at a time when I felt my lowest. Your cakes, fruit salads, smile, and conversation always brought me a higher vibration. Second, I want to thank my soul sister for coping with my psychosis in the most open and caring manner I could have ever asked for. I remember the first time I opened up to you about what I was going through, and you couldn't have handled it any better, my love. You didn't give up on me but sought refuge with me no matter what I was going through. You were and still are my rock.

Third, I want to thank my publisher, editor, and everything in one girl, Kaitlyn, who helped this book take shape. You believed in me when I had no belief in myself and brought my dream come true. You did all the handy work you could do when I felt blue and poured your soul into my work, which I am forever grateful for.

Now I want to thank my mother and sister, and godparents from a distance, who still checked in on me every day. The distance between us was hard to have during such a struggling time, but you all managed to manifest your positive energy over to me on days when I felt like giving up.

I want to give a big thank you to my university friends who gave me a feeling of love and acceptance when I felt lonely and torn up - thanks for the package and your constant checking up on me - not sure what I would've done without it. Thanks to my one and only yogi, Beth, who went through this book for me and was able to put her magic touches on it. You are my star, sister. Also, Valentina, who went over my script and said everything is fantastic when I thought everything I produced was crap at a time of defeat and depression - you spurred me to publish it still!

I'd also like to thank my other friends, including my angels, Holly and Myriam. You both checked up on me consistently and accepted that I wouldn't reply at times of deep distress, but all the while didn't give up on re-sparking my light within - thank you.

All my other friends - you know who you are! I am forever grateful for your guidance and support in the most challenging time in my life.

Drawings done in the mental clinic with Juliane Kraemer.

If you enjoyed this book, then you can find more peace by having a free discovery call with Grace today. Find out what suits you.

www.gracegrossmann.com

Printed in France by Amazon
Brétigny-sur-Orge, FR